The Practical Guide to High School

Campus Ministry

The Practical Guide to High School
Campus Ministry

Constance Fourré
Adrian Mison Fulay
Sandra Iwanski
Roy Petitfils

saint mary's press

The publishing team included Steven C. McGlaun, development editor; Lorraine Kilmartin, reviewer; manufacturing coordinated by the prepress and production services departments of Saint Mary's Press.

Printed in the United States of America

ISBN 978-0-88489-963-1

1346

Library of Congress Cataloging-in-Publication Data

    The practical guide to high school campus ministry / Constance Fourre ... [et al.].
    p. cm.
ISBN 978-0-88489-963-1 (pbk.)
    1. Church work with young adults—Catholic Church. 2. Church work with teenagers—Catholic Church. 3. Church leadership. 4. Catholic high school students—Religious life. I. Fourré, Constance.
BX2347.8.Y64P73 2007
259'.23088282—dc22

                                                        2006028020

Contents

About the Authors

Constance Fourré is the director of faith formation at Benilde–Saint Margaret's School in Saint Louis Park, Minnesota. She has taught at Benilde–Saint Margaret's for sixteen years, with particular emphasis in the areas of service, spirituality, and nonviolence. She has volunteered for many years, teaching English as a second language (ESL) and serving as a community educator on domestic violence. Constance has a bachelor of arts degree in theology from the College of Saint Benedict in Saint Joseph, Minnesota, and a master of arts degree in curriculum and instruction from the University of Saint Thomas in Saint Paul, Minnesota.

Adrian Mison Fulay is the director of campus ministry at Saint Mary's College High School in Berkeley, California. For more than twelve years, he has taught in the religious studies department, with special emphasis in the areas of the Scriptures, rituals, and world religions. He is active in parish work, ministering as director of liturgy for Saint Paschal Baylon Church in Oakland, California. He has also assisted several dioceses in coordinating large diocesan celebrations and liturgies. Adrian has a master's degree in theology from the Jesuit School of Theology in Berkeley.

Sandra Iwanski brings more than thirty years of experience to her role as a pastoral minister. She holds a master of arts degree in pastoral ministries from Saint Mary's University of Minnesota in Winona, Minnesota. She is a local and national consultant and presenter in the areas of parish leadership, adult faith formation, women's spirituality, and catechesis. Currently she chairs the theology department and serves as campus minister for Rosary High School in Aurora, Illinois. Sandra also serves as associate director for the Institute in Pastoral Ministries at Saint Mary's University of Minnesota.

Roy Petitfils teaches theology at Saint Thomas More Catholic High School in Lafayette, Louisiana, where he previously coordinated the campus ministry program. He has served in various capacities during more than ten years of working with young people in parish, college, and high school settings. He holds a bachelor of arts degree in liberal arts from Saint Joseph Seminary College in Saint Benedict, Louisiana. He has studied theology at the graduate level for two years. He is currently completing a master of education degree in community counseling at the University of Louisiana in Lafayette.

Campus Ministry
Introduction and Overview

Within the bustle of a vibrant school environment and among the hectic schedules of the students, faculty members, staffers, and families, campus ministers face the task of inviting others to make time and space for God. No one program or one person can meet all the pastoral needs of a Catholic high school. Instead, meeting those needs takes the involvement of student leaders, faculty volunteers, parents, and a wide range of programs such as retreats, liturgy, and service learning. True campus ministry involves just that—the entire campus. Identifying, therefore, the various aspects of dynamic, comprehensive pastoral programs is essential if campus ministers are to invite the students and faculty members to embrace the call to fullness of life in Christ and in the Church.

A comprehensive campus ministry program includes liturgy and prayer, service learning, retreat ministry, student leadership, and the spirituality of the ministers. Each chapter of *The Practical Guide to High School Campus Ministry* provides a theological framework and explains the various elements of a particular component followed by practical ideas, suggestions, and resources to help you enhance those elements.

These fundamental components will be the "salt" of your pastoral plan. The purpose of salt is to enhance the flavors already present in a dish. Adding too much or not enough salt will take away from the essence of the meal. In the same way, these fundamental components alone will not make your campus ministry great. Their purpose is to enhance the distinctive personality, charism, and identity that are already present in your school.

At its core, campus ministry is about building the Kingdom of God. The means to that end can include program elements such as retreats, liturgies, and service learning. Campus ministry, however, also includes less obvious elements such as the ministry of presence, outreach to families, and advocacy on behalf of the students in administrative discussions. If you are active in campus ministry, you already know the truth that more always remains to be done. There is always another student to reach out to, another contract with a retreat center to complete, or another meeting to attend. For this reason, campus ministers must not enter into the ministry alone. For campus ministry to be truly life changing, it must be a priority of the entire school.

Campus ministers of the new millennium are no longer "lone rangers," but rather pastoral presences on campus. They are part of the faculty and administrators who have embraced the call to make Christ's presence felt in the world through prayer, service, leadership, and spiritual formation.

The goal of this book is to put forth the fundamental elements of comprehensive pastoral ministries in Catholic high schools. As you read each chapter, consider which component or components you might be able to add to, or enhance within, your ministry. This book is not meant to be a definitive, exhaustive work on Catholic high school campus ministries. As you delve into the pages of this book, you may recognize certain components you wish to add to your program. Perhaps you already have a comprehensive program and will find certain suggestions that can enhance an already thriving ministry. The size of your ministry or the number of components in place is not as important as your willingness to use to their full potential whatever resources God has placed at your disposal.

Keep in mind that this book has been created for you to refer to over and over again. Consider marking certain pages you want to come back to and writing notes as you go along. No rule says you have to read it from beginning to end. Feel free to jump around to sections that seem most valuable to you whenever you need to. Note that experienced campus ministers and former campus ministers who understand school life and ministry have put this book together. The authors have made mistakes and enjoyed successes, just as you have, and have learned certain principles and practices that, when adapted well, work in any setting.

The authors of this book come from the expansive field of high school campus ministry, with strong programs in their respective areas. The authors also bring a variety of backgrounds and experiences to their ministries. Through trial and error, they have learned what works well for their communities. They hope this book will serve as a resource to assist in the glorious, trying, and wonderful calling that is campus ministry.

> May God, our loving Creator, guide your words and actions so you might be a light for those in need of hope, a rock for those in need of strength, and a comfort for those in need of compassion.

> May Christ, our Savior, embrace you and enliven you in your ministry so all you do proclaims his glory.

> May the Holy Spirit, our Advocate, find a dwelling place in your heart so you may act for justice, lead with wisdom, and proclaim the Good News with passion.

Chapter 1

Comprehensive Campus Ministry

Developing comprehensive ministry programs is difficult, takes time, and is extremely important if your goal is to reach out to as many students as possible, using the resources at your disposal. A comprehensive ministry is not simply one program existing alongside other equally good programs a school offers. It is, rather, an approach to ministry that develops and nurtures a rich and diverse collection of ministries that serve an equally diverse school community. A comprehensive ministry is a series of relationships sewn into the very fabric of school life and, as such, permeates every function and every organization and has the potential to positively affect every member of the school. A comprehensive approach purposefully calls forth the gifts of the community and uses them to bring Christ's presence into the world in powerful and creative ways.

This holistic approach to pastoral life requires intentionally and systematically reaching out to different sections of school communities. Although building trust and rapport with the students is essential, seeking to include staff and faculty members, alumni, and parents as partners in a shared ministry is equally important. Empowering these groups to help carry out your school's religious mission helps the school achieve its full potential by being a good steward of the resources at its disposal.

As you involve more adults in your programs, whether by inviting them to be leaders on retreat or by asking them to help with service projects, you will develop their ministry and leadership skills. After a while, certain individuals will be obvious choices to invite into leadership roles in the ministry. When you invite others to share leadership responsibilities, large or small, you must set clear expectations on both sides of those relationships. Those leaders need to know what to expect from you, and you need to know what to expect from them. As you continue to invite more adults to share leadership, you will spend more time training, mentoring, and empowering them to be with the students. This can be difficult if you see yourself as the campus minister and not as the coordinator of ministry. For many campus ministers, this paradigm shift from minister to coordinator is the first step in developing a more comprehensive approach. Involving others in actively participating in the shared ministry of the Church is not *preparation* for Christian ministry; it is the *heart* of that ministry. In his book *Campus Ministry,* Keith Warrick presents eight basic concepts underlying campus ministry (see resource 1–A), as well as six objectives for campus ministry. It is beneficial to look at these six objectives, as follows:

1. To communicate and proclaim the gospel message

2. To provide opportunities for members of the school community to deepen their understanding of, and commitment to Jesus, and his message

3. To invite and encourage involvement in and celebration of the faith community through various forms and styles of worship

4. To foster the total personal and spiritual growth of each person
    a. To help individuals realize their significance in relationship to school, family, Church, and world community
    b. To call on and encourage members of the school community to share their gifts and to minister to others' needs by responsible participation in the life, mission, and work of the Church

5. To raise consciousness about, and encourage action regarding contemporary moral and social problems, as well as to urge people to work toward a more just, safe, and peaceful world

6. To complement the general goals and objectives of the religion department and of the school

(Pp. 20–21)

The Practical Guide to High School Campus Ministry was envisioned with these six objectives in mind. Within this book, we will examine the following five components of a campus ministry program: prayer and liturgy, service learning, retreats, leadership development, and the spirituality of the minister. The appendix lists additional resources for you to use in developing and implementing your school's campus ministry programs.

Prayer and Liturgy

Campus ministry programs, as expressions of the ministry of the Church, foster the faith development of entire school communities. Central to the development of Christian faith are experiences of prayer and worship. Catholic schools are called to be communities of faith where prayer and worship shape and transform all their members. (See chapter 2.)

Through meaningful liturgy and prayer experiences, we can deepen the faith of the students and move them more fully into discipleship. Liturgy and prayer remind us of our dependence on God and call us into active worship and dialogue with our Creator. The rituals and traditions of the Catholic faith bless Catholic schools, and it is vital to invite the students into the Church with a delicate balance of Tradition and appropriate adaptations. By involving the whole person—body, mind, and soul—and respecting and using the diversity of the community and the Church, campus ministries can provide liturgy and prayer experiences that reflect the community and move everyone involved closer to God. In chapter 2, you will find an exploration of these topics, as well as planning tools for the celebration of Eucharistic liturgies and prayer.

Service Learning

Catholic high schools provide the students with powerful but less obvious paths to God in their service programs. Many young people who have trouble focusing at the Eucharist, or Mass, or focusing during class discussions are touched by the face of Jesus in people they serve. While doing service, the students step outside their normal routines and encounter adults who display courage and generosity in the face of adversity or children who laugh and play in the midst of suffering. (See chapter 3.)

Service has long been a part of ministry with young people. There is a difference between service and service learning. Chapter 3 explores how service learning, as part of campus ministry programs and incorporated in the curriculum when possible, can move the students beyond direct service into justice work. Through service learning, we can provide the students with a deeper understanding of the issues that threaten the God-given dignity of all people. The learning process culminates in the students' being invited to accept their individual and collective responsibility to creatively and courageously respond to these issues. In addition, the necessary elements of a service learning program are presented, along with a few planning tools.

Retreats

Of the various programs within Catholic high school campus ministries, retreats are among the most important and intricate. Well-done retreats can be some of the most effective tools campus ministers use to bring the students to Christ. As such, retreats are foundational to the pastoral life of Catholic high schools. (See chapter 4.)

Retreats afford the students, along with faculty and staff members, time for solitude with God, conversion and reconciliation, and the development of community. As you read through chapter 4, you will find not only a step-by-step process exploring the various aspects of retreats but also tools to help you address the numerous tasks for implementing successful retreats. You will also find resources to assist you in planning retreats and training retreat teams.

Leadership Development

There are plenty of gifted prayer leaders, creative retreat planners, and students who choose to be dedicated to community service. As a campus minister, you have the particular privilege of discovering, forming, and empowering those student leaders. Together, you and your student leaders can enable your school community to express its connection to God in ways that make sense. In addition, you are in a unique position to set the stage for a lifetime of leading and learning. (See chapter 5.)

By developing and nurturing leaders among the students, faculty and staff members, and alumni of their schools, campus ministers can achieve two goals. First, by inviting others into leadership in ministry, campus ministers can better meet the needs of their communities. No campus minister can be everywhere and do everything. Empowering others creates programs that truly respond to the needs of their schools. Second, by inviting the students into ministerial leadership, campus ministers better equip the students for leadership in the Church and in the larger community. In chapter 5, you will find a more thorough exploration of the importance of leadership development, as well as practical planning tools for finding, training, and empowering leaders.

Spirituality and the Daily Life of the Minister

Ministry in Catholic school settings can be stressful, frustrating, exhilarating, and personally enriching. In the same day, it is possible to experience the most rewarding and challenging moments of your career. With all their ups and downs, twists and turns, campus ministries are a lot like roller coaster rides, delivering unexpected surprises at every turn. Your ministry will call on all the emotional and spiritual resources you possess and will challenge you to acquire even more. (See chapter 6.)

Amid the retreats, meetings, budgets, phone calls, and countless other things that demand the time and attention of campus ministers, losing sight of your own spiritual needs is easy. Among the list of things to do, nurturing your own faith life is vital. Campus ministers are in a position to give of themselves without ceasing. For this reason, many campus ministers burn out and leave the ministry or find themselves just going through the motions of their jobs without passion. In chapter 6, you will find tips on nurturing your own spirituality, as well as some pointers that address such topics as vacation and personal retreats.

Campus Ministers as Coordinators of Campus Ministry

In the majority of Catholic high schools, a person or group of people is designated as the campus minister or ministers. A more appropriate title is actually coordinator of campus ministry. In reality, no one person or small group of people can adequately meet the ministerial needs of a community as large and diverse as a Catholic high school. The task of all campus ministers is to empower members of the community—faculty and staff members, the students, graduates, and parents—to be the campus ministers.

One of the traps many campus ministers fall into is to become lone rangers. In this scenario, the persons designated as campus ministers take on not only the coordination but also all the hands-on aspects of their ministries. Among organizing the daily prayers, providing spiritual direction for the students, assembling liturgical environments for the school, and leading retreat teams, campus ministers are eventually taxed beyond their ability and are unable to see any of the tasks to the optimum outcome.

Catholic high schools have diverse populations and require a variety of personalities, skills, and experiences to meet their ministerial needs. Campus ministers must recognize their gifts and limitations and direct a significant amount of their energy empowering others to be campus ministers, especially others whose talents complement those lacking in the coordinators. Effective ministers understand the importance of enlisting the support of those whose gifts buttress the ministers' weaknesses, thereby enhancing the diversity and scope of their ministries. Saint Paul reminds us to be grateful for the role we can play within Christ's body and to allow others to play their parts. When we minister this way, we are free to spend more time in our areas of strength, while giving others the opportunity to do the same.

Faculty and staff members, the students, graduates, and parents possess abundant time and talents. Effective campus ministers invite others into ministry, provide training and support for volunteers, and facilitate the execution of the various components of their campus ministry programs. This does not mean campus ministers are not involved with their communities. Instead, this style of campus ministry means campus ministers are free to be present to their communities in ways that are not possible when they are the sole workers in the field.

Ministry of Presence

One ministry within the school cannot be programmed. It is the intangible ministry of presence. Campus ministers must have a presence around the school during normal school hours and, when possible, at events that occur outside the school day. The ministry of presence is simply what it sounds like. It is taking the time to walk the halls between classes, touching base with the students. It is spending time in the library, discussing the day's events with the students during their off periods. It is attending a junior varsity basketball game so the students can see you truly care. In the hectic, day-in and day-out activity of a school, losing sight of this simple, yet important, role of campus ministers is easy.

Through having a presence in the school, you are better able to connect with the students, faculty members, and staff, add credibility to the campus ministry program, and become more aware of the pulse of the community and the effect your ministry program has on the school. Through the ministry of presence, you will more easily identify the students ready for involvement in ministry who might otherwise be missed. In addition, you will have the opportunity to minister to young people who would never come to your office seeking assistance.

You can achieve a ministry of presence only when you see it as a priority, rather than as something to be done once all of your "real work" is complete. Touching base with young people in the halls is the work of campus ministers. Checking in on faculty and staff members on their breaks is the job of campus ministers. From a purely programming perspective, personal invitations to be involved can produce more volunteers than countless announcements and e-mails. Also, identifying students in need of assistance by walking through the cafeteria after school is more valuable than keeping office hours, waiting for the students to seek you out.

As a campus minister, you have the calling to be present to the community in a manner that is not open to or expected of other faculty and staff members. By recognizing that part of your job description is to seek out the students, faculty members, and staffers where they spend their time, it is easy to see how your ministry should extend beyond the walls of your office and the confines of programmed events and into the building of relationships with members of the school.

Christian ministry is all about relationships. Jesus always ministered within the context of relationships. He had deeper friendships with those key individuals he selected, and he empowered them to do the same. In the same way, campus ministers, as ministers of presence, gradually but purposefully seek to build relationships with the students, faculty and staff members, administrators, and parents. Within the context of healthy boundaries, campus ministers are able to share the Good News in ways that are personal, relevant, and authentic. Although programs are necessary and important, the students will never be able to connect with programs. The connections that give ministry vitality always happen within relationships. As such, our programs should lead us into, and draw from, the power of our relational ministry of presence.

In the end, the ministry of presence is the heart of Christian ministry. It was the ministry of Christ, who chose to spend time with people. In both formal and informal situations, Jesus modeled the importance of being accessible and visible to those among whom he ministered.

An Incomplete Ministry

Campus ministry, like all ministries within the Church, is incomplete. Around every corner of your school are new opportunities for outreach. There is always a new group of ninth graders who do not know the charism of your school. There will be crises each semester for which complete advance planning is impossible. What works for your school community for daily prayer one year will not work sometime in the future. Campus ministry is incomplete and, therefore, always growing. In providing the direction for the campus ministry program at your school, you have a wonderful opportunity to embrace this incompleteness. In embracing the incompleteness, the campus ministry at your school can grow in remarkable ways. Reach out to new leaders, seek new experiences for your students, embrace what is wonderful in your ministry, and challenge yourself, faculty and staff members, and the students to build a community that proclaims the glory of God.

Eight Basic Concepts Underlying Campus Ministry

Campus ministry is a ministerial complex of pastoral, catechetical, educational, evangelizing, counseling, and prophetic efforts that seeks to build a living faith community.

This definition conveys the sense of a coordinated, holistic ministry effort. It is a ministry that involves the entire faith community of a school: faculty, students, staff, parents, administrators, pastors, and everyone else who is associated with the school. While campus ministry's primary focus is on students, the personal growth and faith development of each person in the school contributes to achieving its fundamental goal of building up and living in a faith community. . . .

The following eight basic concepts are offered to further contribute to a perception of high school campus ministry as a ministerial complex involving a variety of activities, carried out by many different people, and coordinated by a campus minister. . . .

1. Campus ministry, like any ministry, has its fundamental roots in the mission and ministries of the Church. As such, it recognizes the ministerial gifts and the particular charisms of members of the community and calls people forward to share those gifts and charisms in ministering to and with other members of the community.

2. Campus ministry actively responds to the invitation of the Church to extend the Kingdom of God in the world through offering service to those in need and acting on behalf of justice.

3. Campus ministry works to foster the total personal and spiritual growth of each person in the faith community. It is a ministry to, for, by, and with young people, as well as a ministry to the membership of the entire community—faculty, staff, parents, families, administrators, and others. Campus ministry not only deliberates on problems of young people and adults, but it also encourages and enables people to actively participate in resolving them. In other words, campus ministry seeks to draw people to responsible participation in the life, mission, and work of the Church within the context of the school faith community.

4. Campus ministry is a pastoral activity concerned with the total faith development of the individual, respecting one's social and psychological needs as well as one's religious needs. It includes catechesis and incorporates the diverse components that constitute catechesis, that is, sharing faith, experiencing liturgical worship, participating in Christian service and doctrinal instruction.

5. Campus ministry includes and builds upon the process of evangelization. It reaches out, invites, and welcomes people into the life of the school faith community.

6. Campus ministry is a dimension of total religious education. It works at creating an environment in which the student can become more fully human and more fully Christian. Campus ministry works in cooperation with the school's religion department to provide an experiential and voluntary dimension to the religious formation and faith development of students and others in the school.

7. Campus ministry works within the boundaries of an educational institution. Therefore, it is concerned with the overall school philosophy, curriculum, programs, and policies insofar as they all impact the faith community.

8. Finally, the context for campus ministry is the school faith community. Campus ministry works at and supports all faith community building efforts within the school as well as in the extended community of parish and neighborhood.

Chapter 2

Prayer and Liturgy

Overview

Campus ministry programs, as expressions of the ministry of the Church, foster the faith development of entire school communities. Central to the development of Christian faith are experiences of prayer and worship. Catholic schools are called to be communities of faith where prayer and worship shape and transform their members. Every experience of prayer and worship has the capacity to form young people into better Christians by celebrating and deepening their relationships with Jesus Christ. Whether on retreats or in classrooms, during times of sadness or joy, at service projects, during the feast days of the liturgical year, or at the many times when entire schools gather for particular needs, prayer and worship transform young people into disciples who put faith into action in their school communities and in the world.

Liturgy comes from a Greek term meaning "work of the people." Liturgy is the public communal worship act of the Church. Through the rituals, words, and symbols used in worship, God and humanity come together. *Liturgy* is a general term. It can refer to the Eucharistic celebration—Mass—but it can also refer to the Liturgy of the Hours, which is the public prayer of the Church throughout the daily cycle of life. The celebrations of the sacraments, which can take place outside Mass, are also liturgies—for example, the sacraments of Baptism, Anointing of the Sick, Matrimony, or Penance and Reconciliation. Schools can celebrate the Liturgy of the Hours through morning prayer (lauds) or evening prayer (vespers). A school celebration of the word of God is also considered a liturgical act. Other services, though also public and communal expressions of worship, are not necessarily official acts of the Church, so they may or may not be called liturgies.

Prayer, whether personal or communal, recognizes God's presence and action in the world. Prayers of thanksgiving recognize that God is the source of all good things. Prayers of intercession recognize that God provides for all needs. Prayers for forgiveness recognize the eternal mercy and compassion of God. Worship and prayer are expressions of faith, and through expression, faith is nourished.

Providing opportunities for school communities to gather in worship and prayer is an essential purpose of the campus ministry programs of Catholic schools. Through communal expressions of worship, school communities proclaim their faith publicly, while deepening their identities as communities of faith. Personal prayer provides opportunities for individuals to reflect on their relationships with

God and to deepen their faith. Both the personal and the communal expressions of faith and worship serve to enrich the other. "The symbols and rituals of liturgy become more meaningful for young people when they draw from their experiences of private prayer. Likewise, private prayer is revitalized by meaningful experiences of liturgy" (USCCB, *Renewing the Vision*, p. 45).

Campus ministers play critical roles in the development of faith communities by preparing opportunities for prayer and worship with young people that are both formative and transformative. Most important, campus ministers are role models. Before all else, campus ministers must themselves be people whose own prayers and worship shape and deepen their lives. Campus ministers are guides who assist the students in preparing opportunities of prayer and worship that can lead others to a deepening of their faith. They are resources to the students, providing examples or models of prayer and worship from the rich heritage of the Church. As advocates, campus ministers encourage young people to create prayer and worship experiences that use language and styles that can speak to the young people. As organizers, campus ministers oversee the work of many groups and assist in unifying elements and ideas into prayerful experiences for the community. As teachers, campus ministers ensure that the students and their school communities learn and grow from their experiences. In collaboration with the religious studies programs of their schools, campus ministers catechize their school communities. Catechesis and instruction to prepare the students for worship and catechesis after those experiences encourage full and active participation. Finally, campus ministers serve the needs of their school communities, being servants for unity between the needs and concerns of the students and those of administrators and other adults. In those various capacities, campus ministers exercise important roles in working with the students so together, they can prepare experiences of prayer and worship that are true expressions of faith.

Theology

When Christians gather for worship, the main focus and theme of the gathering is always the Paschal mystery—the death and Resurrection of Jesus Christ. Liturgies commemorate not just ideas or feelings but also a life-giving event and a life-giving person. Communities gathered in worship look to a past event but also make that event present, here and now, in the power of the Holy Spirit. In liturgy, Christians look to the coming of Christ in glory. Through liturgy, communities—nourished by the word of God and by the body and blood of Christ—are sent forth to work for the building up of God's Kingdom.

The story of the disciples on the road to Emmaus (Luke 24:13–35) serves as a model for understanding liturgy. In that story, the disciples encounter the risen Christ in his opening of the Scriptures for them and in the breaking of the bread. With hearts on fire from the encounter with the risen Christ, they are compelled to run and tell others the Good News. In essence, this is the heart of liturgy—

that reflecting on the word of God and feasting on the Eucharist, disciples are sent out to proclaim, in word and action, the Good News. Ministry to young people seeks to open the Scriptures, the story of God's great love and promise, and to name that same story at work in their lives. Ministry to young people seeks to open their eyes to the presence of Christ, who is life and love, in their lives today. Ministry to young people seeks to provide experiences whereby those young people encounter the risen Christ so that they, in turn, may share this Good News with others. Prayer and worship with young people provide structured experiences where relationships with Christ can deepen.

The New Testament abounds with stories of Jesus welcoming the lost and the outcast and sharing meals with them. To be fully engaged in the life of the Church, young people must be engaged in worship. Liturgy is the "summit toward which the activity of the Church is directed; at the same time it is the font from which all the Church's power flows" (*Constitution on the Sacred Liturgy* [*Sacrosanctum Concilium*, 1963], no. 10). In the Eucharist, Christians celebrate the presence of the risen Christ in their gathered assemblies, in the one who presides, in the Scriptures proclaimed, and in the bread and wine transformed by the Holy Spirit. This is truly an awesome gift. Participation in the liturgical life of the Church deepens the awareness of this gift. In *From Age to Age: The Challenge of Worship with Adolescents*, the National Federation for Catholic Youth Ministry (NFCYM), notes that many young people experience pressures—developmental, societal, or peer—that prevent them from taking active roles in faith experiences or in liturgical celebrations. Many do not always feel involved in the life of the Church. The challenge of including adolescents in the faith life of the Church is constant. Campus ministers, pastors, youth ministers, and other church ministers must always find ways to invite young people into a deeper awareness and appreciation of their faith. By having their gifts and talents included in vibrant experiences of prayer and worship, young people's life experiences are honored, and their growing and developing faith is respected.

In liturgy, the Church desires "full, conscious and active participation" from the assembled faithful (*Constitution on the Sacred Liturgy*, no. 14). In working with young people to prepare liturgies, campus ministers must provide opportunities where the young people can fully, actively, and consciously participate. Allowing young people to share their gifts and talents with their communities empowers them to take active roles in the life and ministry of the Church.

All liturgies with youth demand their active leadership and participation in preparing the liturgies, their involvement in various liturgical ministries, and the use of their gifts and charisms in the areas of music, art, symbols, and rituals. By understanding and appreciating rituals, the young people can put their experiences of life—friendships, fears, trust, angers, sorrows, and joys—into a ritual language they can share with their peers and the Church through worship.

Preparing Liturgical Celebrations: General Principles

In preparing liturgies and other experiences of prayer and worship with young people, keep in mind the following principles:

- **Liturgical prayer and worship are primarily about God.** Prayer and worship are not just gatherings or school assemblies about particular topics or themes. The whole activity of worship is directed toward God, who is mysteriously transcendent and, at the same time, immanent. In worship, we take time to remember that we are in the holy presence of God. God is always present, but in worship, we focus our particular attention on that holy presence. Every aspect of liturgy, from the readings to music and actions, should focus attention on God's presence in the midst of the gathered assemblies.

- **Ritual prayer and worship involve a delicate balance of elements from Catholic Tradition and appropriate adaptation.** Rituals employ repeated patterns, words, and actions. Some of these have been passed on as part of the rich heritage of the Church. While being attentive to and respecting the Church's heritage, it may at times be necessary to be flexible, creative, and adaptable to meet the needs of the assemblies. This balance between Tradition and adaptation, when achieved, creates experiences of prayer and worship that can truly speak to the participants, at the same time serving as a respectful expression of the larger community of faith.

- **Liturgy and public prayer involve the whole person—body, mind, and spirit.** Listening, singing, and engaging with symbols, postures, gestures, silences, reflection, prayers, and music are just a few of the ways by which participants are engaged in worship. Christians do not worship just from the head up.

- **Ritual prayer and worship integrate various elements into a unified whole.** All the elements of rituals—readings, songs, music, symbolic actions, and so forth—need to flow into, and from, each other in a unified manner. The elements of ritual should complement, and harmonize with, each other. There will be high points and lower points during the ritual, and some elements may be more important than others, but they should form an organic and discernible unity.

- **Ritual prayer and worship pay attention to the diversity that exists in the gathered assemblies.** Participants in the celebrations may come from a diversity of cultures, socioeconomic statuses, ages, and ways of life. Pay careful attention in preparing celebrations so the use of language, symbols, music, imagery, art, and gestures can speak to, and respect, people's diverse experiences. Diversity of roles is also important. Not all students are singers or artists. However, a varied group of talented students should be invited and encouraged to use their gifts for the service of God's people.

These principles of ritual form a basic framework in preparing celebrations of the Eucharist, the word of God, the Liturgy of the Hours, or other celebrations, such as a prayer service commissioning the students who are about to leave for an immersion trip.

Resource 2–A, "Preparing a Eucharistic Celebration (Sample)," and resource 2–B, "Preparing a Prayer Service (Sample)," provide filled-in examples of planning sheets for these celebrations. Resource 2–C, "Preparing a Eucharistic Celebration," and resource 2–D, "Preparing a Prayer Service," are blank forms for these same liturgical celebrations.

Practical Steps in Preparing Liturgical Celebrations

All public celebrations of prayer and worship require careful preparation and planning. The following steps can assist in preparing communal experiences of prayer and worship.

Step One: Using Prayer

The first phase in preparing or creating a prayer or worship experience is to begin with prayer. Gather the student leaders and pray. Those who prepare prayer for others should be shaped by their own prayer life.

Step Two: Determining Purpose

Determine or discuss the purpose and focus of the ritual. If the celebration is a Eucharist, begin by looking at the appointed readings for the day or the feast. Discuss with the liturgy team the liturgical season or the feast to be celebrated. Read the appointed readings with the students and, together, draw out a unifying focus, using the following questions:

- How does the liturgy of this feast day help us better understand Jesus's death and Resurrection?
- What do the readings have in common?
- What are some dominant images from the readings?
- What do the readings and the feast day say to us, our school, or our world today?

Other considerations include the following:

- Information on the cultural and historical background of the reading from a biblical commentary can help bring clarity and insight to the reading.
- Reflections of the group should be shared with the presiding priest to aid in crafting the homily.
- If no readings are assigned or appointed, reflect on the purpose and focus of the liturgy. Once the focus of the celebration is determined, consult the many options provided in the *Lectionary* or consult a Bible commentary, concordance, or list of readings to assist in choosing appropriate readings.

If the celebration is not Eucharistic but instead is based on a given focus—for example, a Lenten prayer service—discuss the purpose and determine a unifying theme or focus of the celebration, asking the following questions:

- Why is our community gathering for prayer and worship—for a reconciliation service, a commissioning ceremony, a service project, a commemoration of an important event or person, or another special need for the school community?
- What sentence or phrase sums up the reason for our gathering in prayer?
- What is going on in the lives of the students or in the school community that calls for the celebration of public ritual prayer?
- What scriptural passages speak to the purpose of the celebration? (Consult the many options from the *Lectionary*, propose readings to the student leaders, or consult a concordance.)
- What other writings, such as poetry, song lyrics, or short stories, complement the scriptural passages for this celebration? (Although many other types of readings may be meaningful, the Scriptures are central to Christian worship. Other types of readings should supplement the Scriptures, not replace them.)

Step Three: Preparing the Elements of the Celebration

Whether preparing a Eucharistic liturgy or another form of celebration, consider the essential elements that will make up the celebration.

Prepare the Physical Environment

As you prepare the environment of the celebration, ask the following questions:

- Where and when will the celebration take place—in a chapel, a classroom, an auditorium, or a gym?
- How will the physical setup look? Where will the participants sit? Do chairs need to be set up?
- Will sound amplification—microphones, speakers, or a sound mixer—be needed?
- How will the liturgical season be represented—by an Advent wreath, Easter candle, Lenten banners, or the use of the liturgical colors?
- What major objects are needed—altar, ambo, font, or presider's chair?
- What ritual objects and symbols are needed—processional cross, icons, candles, vestments, bread and wine, banners, liturgical vessels, holy oils, ritual books (the *Sacramentary*, the *Lectionary*, or *The Book of the Gospels*), incense, ashes, bowls of water and branches for sprinkling, and so on?

Prepare Music

The purpose of music in worship is to support the prayers of the community. Keeping the purpose and focus of the celebration in mind, determine what music will be appropriate. Ask the following questions:

- Which parts of the celebration will be sung? (Parts of the Eucharist should be sung, such as the acclamations.)
- What musical resources are available—choirs, bands, cantors, or soloists?
- What songs do the musicians and the participants already know? Can others sing the songs? Do particular songs help the assembly pray?
- What ritual actions does the singing support—processions, laying on of hands, or other sacred movements?
- What other audiovisuals should include music?

Craft Other Texts

Aside from the Scriptures that will be proclaimed at the celebration, other texts may be needed to tie the various elements together into a unified whole. To determine which additional texts you might need, ask the following questions:

- Is an introduction or call to worship needed?
- Which prayers will be used? (If the celebration is a Eucharist, certain prayers are already assigned. If they are not, the students have the opportunity to craft their own prayers.)
- What are the prayers for the general intercessions? (Intentions should be written that reflect the needs of the local community and the larger human family.)
- What, if any, instructions need to be given? Does the presider need a script to ensure that the ritual flows smoothly?

Use Sacred Movement

The use of movement, like music, engages the body in the celebration. Like music, movement and drama should serve to enrich the prayers of the participants; movements, gestures, or drama should not be performed for the sake of performance. In preparing for movements and drama, ask the following questions:

- Can a drama or brief skit communicate the message of the Scripture reading?
- What movements or gestures can enrich the celebration?
- How can deliberate movements enhance the processions—the entrance, before the Gospel reading, the presentation of the gifts, Communion, or the recessional?

Gestures that come from our Tradition—such as bowing, standing, kneeling, making the sign of peace, laying on hands, anointing, washing feet, using incense, lighting candles, venerating icons, signing the senses, sprinkling with water, or using processions—speak powerfully when done well. The Eucharist and the other sacraments employ a set series of rituals and gestures. When preparing a prayer service, you may choose to use some of the ritual actions described above. Appropriate use of one or two of these can serve as an effective focus of a prayer service.

Putting It All Together

After discussing the various elements, the next step involves compiling the disparate elements into a coherent structure—the order of service. The many plans, suggestions, and ideas of the working groups need to be crafted into a unified plan for the celebration. The structures of the Eucharist, the Liturgy of the Hours, and the sacraments have been passed down through the ages. Because the patterns of these liturgies are set, the various elements that the students decide on (the readings, music, art, and movements) can just be put into their appropriate places. Other forms of celebration and prayer require an outline. A logical flow of events is important for effective public ritual celebrations. The ritual pattern of gathering, listening to God's word, reflecting on the word, responding in prayer, performing ritual actions, engaging in common or shared prayer, and sending forth is a familiar structure that many types of prayer services share. With appropriate modifications, these same general ritual patterns and structures can be used for many types of celebrations.

Deciding on Specific Tasks and Ministries

Once the order of service has been determined, decide who will be responsible for the various tasks. Create a list of ministers, roles, and responsibilities for the celebration, asking the following questions:

- Who will preside? If the celebration is a Eucharist, has the priest been contacted? Has he been involved in the preparations? If the celebration is not a Eucharist or one of the sacraments, have any students been trained who are gifted leaders of public prayer? Are any students capable of sharing a reflection on the readings at the prayer service?
- Who will request the necessary physical setup for the environment?
- Who will set up and take down the sound system?
- Who will coordinate with the music ministers?
- Who will coordinate with those involved in sacred movement?
- Who will prepare participation aids (song booklets or programs)?
- How will other members of the community be prepared for the celebration (announcements to the school community, information or instructions for staff and faculty members)?
- Who will ensure that the celebration goes smoothly (practice with ministers, give cues, be the troubleshooter—this person has traditionally been called the master of ceremonies)?
- Who will set up and take down the ritual items for the celebration?

- Who will serve as lectors, music ministers, Eucharistic ministers, hospitality ministers, and acolytes or altar servers, and who will take part in the processions?

Students acting as sacristans, lectors, altar servers, and extraordinary ministers of Communion need to be trained in the execution of those ministries and formed in the theology of them. Consult your local diocesan office for diocesan guidelines.

Preparing the Assembly

Before the participants experience the liturgy, preparations may be needed to encourage full, conscious, and active participation. Collaborating with other members of the school community (such as the religious studies faculty members, team members, or administrators), activities can be created to prepare for the liturgy. Ask the following questions:

- Does the music need to be rehearsed with the participants? Do the movements and gestures need to be taught beforehand?
- Can the participants prepare an element of the celebration? For example, a prayer activity in homeroom or religious studies classes centering on the parable of the prodigal son can be read, discussed, and prayed about before a communal celebration of Penance later that week. Classroom resources can be distributed about a particular ritual (for example, the sacrament of Anointing) that will be done at the liturgical celebration on an upcoming retreat.

Reflecting on the Experience

After the liturgy, provide ways in their classrooms for participants to reflect on their experiences through journals or written reflections or class discussions. Engage the students in reflecting on what they saw, heard, liked, and would like to see. Providing resources and opportunities to "unpack" the celebration will help the students grow from their experiences. To aid in reflection, forward any feedback from the students to those who prepared the celebration. Gather once again those who prepared the celebration to reflect on and evaluate the experience they have just presented. After getting feedback from the other participants and ministers, consider the following questions:

- What are your overall thoughts about the experience? What did you hear from others? How do you think the celebration went?
- Did we sustain the focus or theme throughout the celebration? Did the prayers, readings, reflection or homily, music, art, movements, and environment connect to the underlying focus, theme, or purpose of the celebration? Did the prayers, readings, music, art, movements, and environment effectively lead the assembly to prayer? Did the ministers encourage the prayers and participation of the assembly?

- What did we do well? What could we have done better? What should we continue to do? What should we not do again? What needs to be strengthened for our next liturgy?

Finally, take the evaluations into account and learn from them, implementing necessary changes to enrich subsequent experiences of prayer and worship.

Conclusion

Human beings are formed and shaped by their experiences. This is true for young people with prayer and worship. An ever-present challenge for campus ministers is to prepare experiences that shape, form, and deepen the faith of the members of their school communities. The experiences young people have of prayer and worship should draw them deeper into relationships with the God who created them in love, with Christ, who shares their sorrows and joys, and with the Holy Spirit, who blesses them with countless gifts and calls them to share those gifts with others. It is an immense responsibility to prepare celebrations that can accomplish this. Each experience of public prayer and worship should have this goal in mind, because every time young people gather in prayer is a time of formation and transformation. By using young people's gifts, talents, voices, and expressions, and in respecting the work of God in young people's hearts and lives, ministers can assist young people in preparing truly vibrant celebrations that speak to them and their experiences. Vibrant prayer and worship celebrations can draw young people more fully into the life of the Church, that they may be shaped into faithful disciples of the Lord for their schools, their families, and their world.

Preparing a Eucharistic Celebration (Sample)

Initial Preparation

Name of Feast or Special Occasion: . . . . All Saints' Day Liturgy
Date, Time, Location: . . . . November 1, 2007
9:30 a.m.
Main Auditorium
Focus of the Celebration: . . . . "Called into the Communion of Saints"

Preparation of the Students

Earlier in the week, through religious studies classes, the students were asked to reflect on people who have been examples of holiness. Those names were written on stickers, which the campus ministry liturgy prep team put on ribbons and made into banners. Six large ribbon banners will be hung above the assembly. In class, the students also wrote their own litany of saints.

Liturgical Ministers

Presider: . . . . Father Jayson
Hospitality Ministers: . . . . Campus Ministry Student Liturgy Team
Ministers of the Word: . . . . Simone B., Jon T.
Music Ministers: . . . . School chorus
Eucharistic Ministers: . . . . Five students, four faculty or staff
Sacristan: . . . . Levan A.
Worship Aid Prepared By: . . . . Levan A.
Other Ministers: . . Dance ensemble; acolytes: Giselle F., Justin L., Catherine K.

General Description of Environment and Use of Art

Altar in the center of auditorium, ambo by the bleachers, seats facing each other (antiphonal seating) toward the altar. Six ribbon banners hang above the assembly seating. Presider's chair by the ambo. Large painting of saints with candles in the lobby where the students enter.

General Description of the Use of Movement

Dancers lead the procession, clothe the altar, and present gifts.

The Order of Mass
Introductory Rites

Gathering Song: . . . . *We Arise*
Penitential Rite: . . . . Spoken
Glory to God: . . . . *Misa Del Mundo*
Opening Prayer: . . . . From the Feast Day, *Sacramentary*, page 728

The Liturgy of the Word

First Reading. . . . . Revelation 7:2–4,9–14
   Proclaimed By: . . . . .Simone B.
Responsorial Psalm: . . . . "All the Ends of the Earth" (Psalm 98)
   Cantor: . . . . .Eliot N.
Second Reading: . . . . 1 John 3:1–3
   Proclaimed By: . . . . Jon T.
Gospel Acclamation (sung): . . . . *Misa Del Mundo Alleluia*
   Cantor: . . . . .Eliot N.
Gospel Reading: . . . . .Matthew 5:1–12a

Homily
(At times, other ritual elements may take place after the homily: signing with ashes, renewal of baptismal promises, rite of Confirmation, and so on)

Prayers of Petition and Intercession
   Composed By: . . . . Giselle F. and Justin L.
   Read By: . . . .Marc P. and Monica L. with sung refrain after each intention

The Liturgy of the Eucharist

Preparation of the Gifts
   Gifts Presented By: . . . . Dance ensemble
Prayer over Gifts: . . . . From the *Sacramentary*, page 728
The Eucharistic Prayer and Acclamations
Preface: . . . .#71
Holy, Holy, Holy (usually sung): . . . . *Misa Del Mundo*
Eucharistic Prayer: . . . .#EP III

Memorial Acclamation (usually sung): . . . . *Misa Del Mundo*
Great Amen (usually sung): . . . . *Misa Del Mundo*

Communion Rite

Lord's Prayer: . . . . Recited
Sign of Peace
Breaking of the Bread with Litany: . . . . *Misa Del Mundo*
Communion Song: . . . . *O Love of God/Amor de Dios*
Hymn of Praise or Thanksgiving: . . . . None
Prayer After Communion: . . . . From the *Sacramentary,* page 729

Concluding Rite

Blessing: . . . . From the *Sacramentary,* page 729
Dismissal
Recessional Song: . . . . "When the Saints Go Marching In"

Preparing a Prayer Service (Sample)

Initial Preparation

Name of Occasion:. . . . . Advent Liturgy
Date, Time, Location: . . . . .December 2
9:30 a.m.
Main Gymnasium
Focus of the Celebration: . . "Light, Hope, and Peace: An Advent Celebration"

Preparation of the Students

Several of the short readings from the prayer service were distributed in religious studies classes earlier in the week. The students read the passages and wrote reflections on them or prayers inspired by them. These were collected; some of the prayers will be used in the prayer service. Some of the reflections will be printed in the worship aid.

Ministers

Presider: . . . . .Simone B.
Hospitality Ministers: . . . . Campus Ministry Student Liturgy Team
Ministers of the Word:. . . . . .Marie P., Mike W.
Music Ministers:. . . . . .School chorus
Sacristan:. . . . . Levan A.
Other Ministers: . . . Dance ensemble; readers for the reflections; candle bearers

General Description of Environment and Use of Art

Auditorium is darkened. Seats face each other (antiphonal seating) with ambo at one end, the chorus at the other, and the Advent wreath and stand for the lamps in the center. Purple banners hang from the ceiling at each of the four corners. Purple cloths drape the ambo.

General Description of the Use of Movement

Dancers lead the procession and lead the assembly in singing and signing (with simple hand movements) the refrain of the responsorial psalm.

The Order of Service

Opening Rites

Call to Prayer: . . . . .Simone B.
Song: "Mantra of Prepare the Way of the Lord," as procession enters, led by dancers
Opening Prayer: . . . Composed by Campus Ministry Team, read by Simone B.

Readings

First Reading: . . . . Isaiah 11:1–10
    Proclaimed By: . . . . Marie P.
Psalm: . . . ."My Soul in Stillness Waits" (Psalm 95)
    Cantor: . . . . Phillip H.
(Gestures at the refrain, dancers move to the verses.)
Second Reading: . . . . .Luke 1:67–79
    Proclaimed By: . . . . Mike W.

Reflection on the Readings

Shared By: . . . . .Isabelle B.

Ritual Actions

Description of Ritual/Symbolic Actions: Litany of peace and lighting of lamps . . . There are four short readings (quotations from various people). After a short reading, a prayer of hope (written earlier that week by the students in class) is said while a lamp is lit and placed in the center. After each prayer, the candles of the people seated in each section are lit.

Music or Song: . . . . Instrumental

Prayers

    Composed By: . . . . Students in religious studies classes
    Read By: . . . . .Mike H. and Phoebe B.
The Lord's Prayer
Sign of Peace

Closing

Blessing
Sending Forth/Dismissal
Song: . . . . "O Come, O Come Emmanuel"

Preparing a Eucharistic Celebration

Initial Preparation

Name of Feast or Special Occasion:
Date, Time, Location:

Focus of the Celebration:

Preparation of the Students:

Liturgical Ministers

Presider:
Hospitality Ministers:
Ministers of the Word:
Music Ministers:
Eucharistic Ministers:
Sacristan:
Worship Aid Prepared By:
Other Ministers (movement, acolytes, gift bearers):

General Description of Environment and Use of Art:

General Description of the Use of Movement:

The Order of Mass

Introductory Rites

Gathering Song:
Penitential Rite:
Glory to God:
Opening Prayer:

The Liturgy of the Word

First Reading:
    Proclaimed By:
Responsorial Psalm:
    Cantor:

Second Reading:
    Proclaimed By:
Gospel Acclamation (sung):
Gospel Reading:
Homily:
(At times, other ritual elements may take place after the homily: signing with ashes, renewal of baptismal promises, rite of Confirmation, and so on)
Prayers of Petition and Intercession
    Composed By:
    Read By:

The Liturgy of the Eucharist

Preparation of the Gifts
    Gifts Presented By:
Prayer over Gifts:
The Eucharistic Prayer and Acclamations:
Preface:
Holy, Holy, Holy (usually sung):
Eucharistic Prayer:
Memorial Acclamation (usually sung):
Great Amen (usually sung):

Communion Rite

Lord's Prayer
Sign of Peace
Breaking of the Bread with Litany:
Communion Song:
Hymn of Praise or Thanksgiving:
Prayer After Communion:

Concluding Rite

Blessing
Dismissal
Recessional Song:

Preparing a Prayer Service

Initial Preparation

Name of Occasion:

Date, Time, Location:

Focus of the Celebration:

Preparation of the Students:

Ministers

Presider:

Hospitality Ministers:

Ministers of the Word:

Music Ministers:

Sacristan:

Other Ministers:

General Description of Environment and Use of Art:

General Description of the Use of Movement:

The Order of Service

Opening Rites

Call to Prayer

Song:

Opening Prayer:

Readings

First Reading:

    Proclaimed By:

Psalm:

    Cantor:

Second Reading:

    Proclaimed By:

Reflection on the Readings

Shared By:

Ritual Actions

Description of Ritual/Symbolic Actions:

Music or Song:

Prayers

Composed By:
Read By:
The Lord's Prayer
Sign of Peace

Closing

Blessing
Sending Forth/Dismissal
Song:

Chapter 3

Service Learning

Overview

Liturgies, retreats, family prayers, and religion classes all have a share in supporting young people's growth in faith. Catholic high schools provide the students with powerful but less obvious paths to God in their service programs. Many young people who have trouble focusing at the Eucharist or during class discussions are touched by the face of Jesus in people they serve. While doing service, the students step outside their normal routines and encounter adults who display courage and generosity in the face of adversity or children who laugh and play in the midst of suffering. For many students, this is a new and startling manifestation of God's presence. Their discovery should come as no surprise. Many in Church ministry found their first real faith experiences during mission trips, summer immersion experiences, or after-school volunteer work. Service opportunities are both natural expressions of our faith and invitations to experience God in the flesh.

In addition to supporting faith development, service opportunities can help lift young people from depression, give them a sense of meaning and purpose in life, guide them in choosing careers, and allow them to discover talents they did not know they have. Service can give shy students new social opportunities and help all the students glimpse worlds other than their own. Service opportunities provide settings where young people can see that faith is not limited to formal prayer or classroom time but is a part of real life.

Service programs can be structured in a variety of ways. Many schools have Christian service classes, where the focus of the course is service and the students are graded accordingly. Volunteer opportunities can be offered as extracurricular activities. (Technically, service done as a requirement for a course is not volunteering.) Whatever the structure, well-run service programs offer the students a range of opportunities, encourage and guide them in their work, hold them accountable for their commitments, and recognize and celebrate their achievements.

Service Learning

We are all familiar with typical service experiences: collections and fund drives, visits to nursing homes, after-school child care programs, and so on. Service learning is a unique strategy with the power to move these volunteer opportunities beyond simply offering a helping hand to a method of mastering academic content, as well.

The service learning movement has gained momentum over the last twenty years because it holds so much power to help participants learn. Service learning uniquely and deliberately integrates service with learning.

Service Learning Is More than Experiential Learning

Service learning is not simply a natural by-product of service, nor is it the same as experiential learning, which develops hands-on strategies for making education come alive. Many people who call their programs service learning are, in fact, engaging their students in experiential learning. Service learning moves a step beyond experiential learning. It combines real service in the community with structured reflection and integration with a subject to be learned. Service learning helps the students find the answers to the classic and legitimate questions "Why do we need to know this?" and "When am I ever going to use it?"

Experiential learning, for example, could involve assigning the students to interview residents of a nursing home to learn about life during the Second World War. Service learning, on the other hand, might have those students make scrapbooks representing their new knowledge and present them to the residents. Experiential learning might have the students exercise their writing skills by composing basic computer instruction manuals. A service learning approach might have the students write instruction manuals and then work individually with senior citizens, using the manuals as guides. The students get real-life feedback on the quality of their work and find new motivation to write clearly and communicate effectively.

Many experiential learning programs do encourage the students to reflect, although on a fairly basic level. Those students are often invited to journal about their emotional responses to their experiences and perhaps what they have learned or would choose to do differently in future projects. Service learning requires a more structured approach to reflection and a more deliberate connection to learning objectives. Service learning is a superb resource both for helping young people learn theology and for integrating a Catholic perspective across a school's curriculum.

Service learning offers a powerful means for the students to learn about a variety of subjects. In campus ministry programs or theology classes, this means integrating service with the meaning of the Scriptures, the person of Jesus, Catholic social teaching, or any one of a number of other topics. In other disciplines, for example, working in after-school programs with Hispanic children can help motivate the students to learn to speak Spanish fluently and correctly. Monitoring the quality of nearby lakes helps the students learn about ecological systems and precise measurement. Resource 3–A, "Service Learning (Sample One): Catholic

Social Teaching," and resource 3–B, "Service Learning (Sample Two): The Role of Prophets," illustrate two different service learning projects.

Service and the Curriculum

To transform service into service learning experiences, it is important to identify learning objectives is important. In strictly service experiences, the students' learning is spontaneous and fairly haphazard. Sometimes the students' experiences confirm, rather than transform, negative stereotypes they may bring to their work. Carefully designed reflection before, during, and after service experiences can help the students reap the maximum benefits from their work and help them remember and apply their new insights to future endeavors.

An obvious learning objective is deepening an understanding of Catholic social teaching. Service projects in parish or Catholic agencies could help the students learn about the structure of the Church and how it functions. Serving in parishes that serve other cultures can help the students learn about the universality of the Church. Teaching in religious education programs can help the students learn about the Scriptures. Prayerful reflection, with written follow-up, can help the students see God's presence in any service experiences. Serving in domestic abuse agencies can help the students learn about the sacrament of Matrimony in all its complexity. Service in funeral homes or helping with funerals could help the students engage with courses in death and dying.

Making the connection can happen from either end. Sometimes a service experience comes along, and teachers or campus ministers find a connection with course objectives. In other cases, teachers may have well-established courses and can create service learning projects that can illuminate the course content. Simply having the students tutor other students in a subject brings new depth to learning about that subject. Your state department of education may have resources and trainers to help you establish service learning in your school. The National Youth Leadership Council (NYLC) and the National Service-Learning Clearinghouse (NSLC) offer training, while supporting research and providing a wealth of ideas and strategies.

Theological Connection

Both the Scriptures and our Catholic Tradition invite us to serve. From the Book of Genesis through the Gospels, from the *Didache*—one of the earliest known documents of nonscriptural teaching—to the teachings of Pope Benedict XVI, we are called to reach beyond ourselves, care for creation, share our resources, and protect the powerless.

Although some see service as an optional add-on, it is, in fact, the essence of our faith. A school's structure expresses its true perspectives on the issue. Respect for the core importance of teaching the students to serve will be reflected in hiring adequate staffers to establish quality programs.

The Scriptures

The people who lived the Old Testament had a particular sensitivity to the voice of God in their midst. From the very beginning, a sense of responding to God's direction was woven into their views of the world. In Gen. 1:28–31, God sees the goodness of his creation and gives it to humans for their sustenance. Although some have interpreted God's instruction to "have dominion" over creation as a license to exploit it, in fact this passage describes Earth as God's gift to humans. Our current understanding of the finite dimensions of this resource moves us to care for it ever more carefully.

The Jewish people of the Old Testament spent much of their history under oppression, which gave them a keen sense of justice and the plight of the powerless. The Exodus from Egypt is an archetype of God's deliverance of the poor and oppressed from bondage into freedom and the Promised Land. The recurring message of the prophets is to care for widows, orphans, and aliens. God enjoins his people to care for the powerless—Jews and Gentiles alike—and his displeasure is clear when they fail. Through good times and bad, calls to the common good, mercy, and justice prevail. The message is encapsulated in the prophet Micah's admonition to "do justice, and to love kindness, and to walk humbly with your God" (Mic. 6:8).

Young people are not always highly receptive to abstract theology, although knowing Catholic doctrine is certainly an important aspect of Catholic education. What young people need desperately are role models, a sense that God is with them, a felt experience of Jesus's presence as a vital, living person. Encountering God's presence and knowing what it means to be a disciple of Jesus provide the underpinning of service work.

In the New Testament, Jesus calls his followers to lay down our lives and to share what we have with the poor. Jesus's words and, even more powerfully, his example show us and the young people we teach that material things do not hold the key to happiness. In Matthew, chapter 25, Jesus's powerful images of the sheep and the goats are sobering reminders that he intends us to take his message seriously.

In the Acts of the Apostles, the early Church held all things in common. The Church members were known for their care of the poor and their commitment to peace. Acts 4:34 says, "There was not a needy person among them." Such a claim could not be made today, and yet it is a goal for all followers of Jesus.

Church Teaching

From the beginning, Church teaching has echoed this message of Jesus and the prophets. The *Didache* says:

> Be not a stretcher forth of the hands to receive and a drawer of them back to give. If you have anything, through your hands you shall give ransom for your sins. Do not hesitate to give, nor complain when you give; for you shall know who is the good repayer of the hire. Do not turn away

from him who is in want; rather, share all things with your brother, and do not say that they are your own. (Chapter 4)

By example and teaching, the Church throughout the centuries has cared for the poor. Feeding the hungry and caring for the sick have been expected of saints, churches, and monasteries. Although at times, during dark stretches of history, the Church has aligned itself with the powerful, there have always been those believers who are faithful to the message. Particularly in the last century, the Church has shown wise and courageous leadership in speaking out on behalf of justice and compassion.

From *Rerum Novarum* in 1891 to *Deus Caritas Est* in 2006, our popes have declared the essential nature of charity and justice. Pope Benedict XVI describes it in *Deus Caritas Est*:

As the years went by and the Church spread further afield, the exercise of charity became established as one of her essential activities, along with the administration of the sacraments and the proclamation of the word: love for widows and orphans, prisoners, and the sick and needy of every kind, is as essential to her as the ministry of the sacraments and preaching of the Gospel. The Church cannot neglect the service of charity any more than she can neglect the Sacraments and the Word. (No. 22)

Charity and Justice

Much has changed since Jesus preached to the small crowds within reach of his voice. We now live in a global society, and actions in one corner of the world can have important implications for people thousands of miles away.

As our knowledge expands and our world becomes more complex, simply sharing food or clothing is not enough. Even in the Old Testament, the prophets challenged kings to be just, as well as merciful. Particularly over the last century, the teaching voice of the Church has been lifted to challenge structures, as well as individual moral choices.

The Catholic vision of the world embraces the need for both charity and justice. Charity—direct response to immediate needs—is critical in the face of hunger, homelessness, and illness. Action for justice—work to change the structures that allow people to be hungry, homeless, and without access to education and health care—is necessary to prevent those sources of suffering from becoming ever more potent forces in our world. Service learning is a powerful method of helping the students and parents understand the distinction and the importance of that teaching.

In 1998, the American Catholic bishops issued a statement titled *Sharing Catholic Social Teaching: Challenges and Directions, Reflections of the U.S. Catholic Bishops*. This statement forcefully declares that educating people on Catholic social teaching is essential to the Catholic view of faith and the world. They said:

The values of the Church's social teaching must not be treated as tangential and optional. They must be a core part of teaching and formation. . . . Just as the social teaching of the Church is integral to Catholic faith, the social justice dimensions of teaching are integral to Catholic education and catechesis. They are an essential part of Catholic identity and formation.

Charity and justice complement each other—they do not oppose each other. Without charity, people will die of hunger and disease today. Without action for justice, people will continue to be at risk tomorrow. The shorthand version of the distinction is "Give people a fish, and they eat for a day; teach them to fish, and they eat for a lifetime." Taking the analogy one step further, action for justice would also ensure that fishing waters are clean and the supply of fish protected.

A range of service opportunities is available for the students, lying on a continuum between charity and justice. Involving the students in charitable service activities includes engaging them in collections and fund drives and in direct service such as stocking food shelves. Empowering service projects bring the students to personal encounters that engage others in ways that leave those others better able to secure necessary resources for themselves. Those projects help teach skills or help those served find inner resources because of the power of relationships. Forming a child care service or a sewing cooperative for immigrant women or tutoring children to help them improve reading and math skills are equivalent to teaching someone to fish. Teaching your students to advocate for immigration reform or protecting groundwater moves them solidly into action for justice.

Advocating for justice also has the potential to move campus ministers squarely into the middle of controversy. Contrary to popular belief, following Jesus does not necessarily lead to a tame life. Wise justice workers know that some controversy is inevitable. Seasoned justice workers know that much controversy can be avoided by careful attention to relationships, proper preparation, and communication. This is God's work. Some resistance is to be expected. If we lose people because of our tendency to be confrontational, our desire for attention, or our enjoyment of stirring things up, we are responsible for that loss. Mohandas K. Gandhi and Martin Luther King Jr. strategized carefully before taking action. Although making mistakes is normal, learning from them is important. Each school community is unique, and service programs need to be adapted to each situation. Seek a healthy balance between supporting the students and parents and challenging them as they move toward a new vision shaped by Catholic social teaching.

Although communication is always important, it is critical while teaching high school students about advocating for justice. Be sure to keep your administrators, colleagues, and students' parents informed of any actions you intend to take. If you do make a mistake, do what you can to mend the relationships and explain your actions.

Backing up our invitations with Church teaching can be very helpful. Fortunately, we are blessed with an abundance of support in Church documents.

For example, the Web page of the Office for Social Justice of the Archdiocese of St. Paul and Minneapolis is just such a site with easy access to a wide range of resources.

The rewards of advocating for justice are enormous. You will never fully know the implications of engaging the students in this work. When you get tired, take a moment to call to mind a change you have seen in a student or an effort the student began that continues to have long-term results. The chain reactions started by your work stretch far into the future and beyond the scope of your vision.

As a Church, we are called to engage in acts of charity and action for justice. As a Church body, some people may be called to one type of action at given stages in their lives, and others at different stages. As Catholic educators, we have a responsibility to introduce young people to the call and the experience of both charity and justice.

Practical Planning Tools

Coordinating service programs requires a unique blend of flexibility and organization. Honestly assess your own strengths and weaknesses in these two areas and if possible or necessary, find allies in areas where you need added strength.

Relationships

Relationships are at the core of any successful service program. A basic program can require the students to find their own sites, make the connections, and get started on their own. With such a program, you will have a substantial number of students who never get up the nerve to start and others who try hard to connect with an agency that is unresponsive or poorly run. In the long haul, it is most efficient and productive to develop a list of agencies that use the students' time well, can report to you on their progress, and provide safe environments for volunteers.

Your list of agencies can be as simple as a box of 3-by-5-inch cards that the students can use and that you can update as you have time. You can also keep information on a database and print out current listings for the students. What is important is that the contact information is current and that you maintain your list based on feedback from both the students and the agencies.

The students need to understand that their behavior directly affects your school's relationships with those agencies. In particular, the students' failure to appear without giving advance notice can damage an agency's willingness to work with you. Before the students begin, help them understand how much those they serve may be counting on their presence. Help them know appropriate ways of letting agencies or clients know if they have unavoidable time conflicts.

Some service programs allow the students to leave campus during the school day. If yours does, it is extremely important that the students respect the policy and that you hold them accountable. Service programs can stretch a school in terms of potential legal liability and disruption of the school day. Doing everything you can to minimize disruption will maximize the flexibility you are allowed with your program.

Parents can be strong allies in creating and sustaining service programs. They may also have legitimate concerns about programs that are poorly run or that place the students in potentially risky settings. Communication is key to maintaining good relationships with parents. Parents have a right to decide where they will allow their children to serve, even if we might disagree with their decisions.

Family service opportunities hold great potential both for building positive relationships and for creating precious family time. Many teenagers today are overscheduled, running on empty, tired, and cranky when they are at home. Many parents yearn for time to spend with their children other than as spectators at their activities. Family service opportunities can give parents and kids unique time together and help parents see the value of your program and its larger objectives. Parents can be an important help in transporting the students, especially those too young to have driver's licenses.

Selecting Service Projects

Not all service opportunities are equally appropriate or valuable. The students have been known to ask credit for service hours for time spent visiting grandparents, performing in plays, or singing in choir. You need to decide what counts as service if you are recording the hours the students serve. Your parameters may shift as you develop your program. No matter where you place your limits, parents or the students likely will challenge them at some point. A useful guideline can be to require that at least some service hours must involve direct contact with people and move the students outside their familiar worlds. For some, contact with the elderly or with little children is a step outside their comfort zones. Others are ready for more dramatic challenges. Handout 3–A, "Service Project Information," is designed to help service coordinators and the students be better informed about their chosen service opportunities. The students complete their copy of the handout before starting their projects, returning them to the service coordinator.

Some of the most valuable projects require substantially more work on the part of supervisors. Sponsoring a fund drive or collecting toiletry items for a shelter requires only making posters, writing some announcements, and gathering and delivering items. On the other hand, setting up an after-school tutoring program where none exists can require planning and organization, transportation of the students, and your weekly presence. Be realistic about your own time and energy. Campus ministry challenges people to give their all and then some. Serving the poor and vulnerable and helping the students see the value in doing so can require even greater sacrifice. Remember that like Earth, you are a finite resource and take care of yourself accordingly.

If possible, match the students with projects where they are likely to succeed. There is a delicate balance between helping young people stretch and putting them in environments where they will feel overwhelmed and want to quit. Many students need strong support during the first weeks of their project. Putting necessary limits on your program will help you provide that support. Veteran volunteers can sometimes help mentor rookies and get them over any initial rough spots.

Student Safety and Legal Concerns

Maintaining records and making sure permission forms are signed and on file are important, if tedious, parts of successful service programs. Permission forms give you a record of where the students are serving and obviously provide verification that parents have been notified of, and support, their children's activities.

In suburban or rural schools, the students may serve in sites in larger cities, where some standards of behavior may be unfamiliar to them. Some students' and parents' fears about safety may be exaggerated, but at the same time, young people need to be instructed about basic safety precautions.

The students working in unfamiliar neighborhoods or areas with relatively high crime rates need to plan their routes ahead of time. Advise the students to dress appropriately for their sites. The students need to respect those people they encounter, both inside and outside an agency. They should keep to themselves any comments of surprise or dismay and share them later with you or the other students only after leaving or during follow-up discussions. Students should visit some sites only during daytime. Encourage the students to contact supervisors and to ask questions if they are concerned about safety or about responding to clients who may make them uncomfortable.

Some students will serve in settings where people handle conflict or personal space in unfamiliar ways. The students may need help understanding others' behavior and responding in ways that will help them feel safe. There is an important balance between refraining from adding to stereotypes and keeping the students safe. Thoughtful discussions on those issues can help the students gain grounded new insights.

Besides permission forms, you may want to keep records of your students' hours served. This is obviously important if the service program is tied to an academic class. The gold level President's Volunteer Service Award honors the students who have done one hundred or more hours of service in a year. Some schools put service hours on student transcripts. The students can maintain their own records of the hours they have served and turn them in periodically to the service coordinator. Your students can use handout 3–B, "Service Hours Record," to track the time they devote to their service learning projects. Ideally, a person on site can verify the students' presence and evaluate their performance. By spot-checking to verify the student records, you maintain the credibility of your program.

Funding and Staffing

Service programs in many schools are chronically short of funds. Although these programs are not as costly as athletics, for example (a useful comparison to use when advocating for your program), transportation can be expensive. Appropriate staffing also is usually an issue.

If possible, as the program grows, advocate for increased staffing. Jim Hamburge, principal of Judge Memorial Catholic High School in Salt Lake City, Utah, says wisely, "For every dollar I spend on a service program, I can raise ten because of the improved PR for our school." Sometimes, people in ministry take too seriously Jesus's admonition not to let the right hand know what the left hand is doing. We can feel uncomfortable bragging about our program. Consider that we do not toot the horn of our service program out of ego; it is, rather, a way of letting the larger community know the needs of our program and giving them the opportunity to support it.

Blessing and Celebrating

A number of years ago, a Lutheran minister went on a mission trip to Central America. He and his group happened to arrive during a week when the village they were visiting was celebrating an extended feast day. Work on the construction site where the team intended to work was halted for several days. A number of people on the team were frustrated.

One of the leaders of the village looked compassionately at the North American visitors. He shook his head slowly and said with a smile, "Clearly, you are not here for the long haul." Celebration is essential to maintaining this type of work in the proper spirit. We need to take time out to celebrate. Successful service programs can grow exponentially. As community agencies hear of your success, you will receive more and more pleas for help. This is good news, but it can lead to stress and exhaustion. Certainly, many of our students are stressed and exhausted. Celebrating and blessing can transform grim determination to of joy and gratitude.

Service programs can help the students see the value of celebrations and rituals and the opportunities they offer us to invite God into our life experiences. Some of these times can be prayerful, and others can be pure celebration. Food tends to lift the spirits of young people, and simply closing the semester or year with a small party can help make your program memorable.

Stories are important. Give your students a chance to share stories of their work. Their stories will help recruit others to your program and capture moments that will remain in their memories to guide them in the future. Stories are an important asset as you share your program with administrators and parents and ask them for their support.

Having the students share photographs in portfolios, PowerPoint presentations, or posters helps them remember and honor their experiences. Be sure the students ask the permission of those they photograph and perhaps share copies with the people they have met.

Prayer

Prayer, during the year and at its close, can bless the students' experiences and help them see those experiences in new and broader perspectives. Invite the students to pray during their experiences for those they serve and for guidance in difficult situations. They can ask blessings for those they have met and those in the larger world they have glimpsed. The students who work with immigrant children may catch a glimpse of conditions in those children's home countries. The students who work with people with disabilities may realize for the first time that many people live with physical limitations. Prayer can be a way to connect with these larger worlds, to hold them in our hearts and our consciousness.

Remind the students to offer prayers of gratitude, as well as petition. Most fundamentally, time spent in focused prayer reminds the students that God is present in each person, each moment. Using music, images, and spaces prepared for quiet reflection calls God consciously into the students' experiences and offers the best opportunity to make their work truly Christian experiences.

Conclusion

Young people experience God and deepen their faith in numerous ways. Catholic schools are uniquely positioned to provide the students with a range of opportunities to help their faith grow. Service learning embodies the "head, heart, and hands" model of Catholic education by integrating Church teaching, hands-on experiences, and personal challenges.

Authentic service calls the students not only to give of themselves but also to develop a faith-based view of the call to justice. Well-designed service programs help the students begin to understand and build right relationships in their own lives and in the world around them. For young people and adults alike, service responds to Jesus's call to be salt for the earth and light for the world.

Service Learning (Sample One)

Catholic Social Teaching

The most fundamental principle of Catholic social teaching is the essential dignity of the human person. All other principles rest on this basic premise. A faith perspective leads us to see that all human beings deserve respect and care simply because God created them as gifts to the world in this moment.

Our American culture's influence causes some young people to see others as being more or less valuable depending on their age, health, productivity, or other behaviors. Other students who have been sheltered do not realize the ways in which some members of our society are robbed of their dignity. Almost any service project that puts the students in relationships with people who have been marginalized can help the students gain a new appreciation for the real meaning of this principle.

Let us take an example of students working in an after-school program for children from lower-income urban families. In preparation for the project, introduce the principle of human life and dignity and make sure the students understand it intellectually. Ask the students to write down what they expect to see during their project and what challenges and opportunities the experience will afford them. Keep these reflections for future reference.

During the service experiences, the students will observe the behaviors of children, their parents, and the paid staffers who work with them. Help the students distinguish between behaviors they observe and interpretations they may make about what the behaviors mean. For example, the students might observe parents who arrive late to pick up their children and assume this tardiness reflects a lack of care on the part of the parents. The real explanation may be difficulties with transportation or unavoidable delays connected with the parents' work. Reading a chapter from a book such as Jonathan Kozol's *Amazing Grace: The Lives of Children and the Conscience of a Nation* can give the students an inside look at the people they are serving.

Reflections that deliberately tie service experiences to Catholic social teaching could ask questions such as the following:

- In what ways is the children's fundamental dignity affirmed?
- In what ways is their dignity denied?
- How could the agency better serve the needs of its clients and thus support their dignity?
- Does the government support parents who are working and poor in ways that allow them to live in dignity?
- In your project, have you seen human dignity challenged or denied in ways that you have not experienced in your own life?

Close by having the students reread their expectations before the project and note ways they are now more aware of the full humanity of the people they have served.

Service Learning (Sample Two)

The Role of Prophets

At first, Old Testament classes would not seem to lend themselves well to service projects. But throughout much of Jewish history, prophets challenged the people of Israel to change their ways, focus their lives, and care for the poor and powerless in their midst.

Many students still believe that the role of prophets is to foretell the future rather than to challenge people to live in accordance with God's will. Make sure the students understand the more fundamental meaning of a prophet's role and remind them that we still have major and minor prophets in today's world.

Catholic Relief Services (CRS) plays a prophetic role in many places where its workers are present. CRS is the primary relief organization of the Roman Catholic Church. Active in many countries around the world, its workers engage in direct relief and work for structural change. They have an excellent reputation for delivering services under difficult circumstances, and the students can be proud of this organization's witness to the world. CRS has an excellent Web site that explains the group's work and gives solid information on the circumstances and structures the group encounters. Have the students explore the CRS Web site and select one country or topic to explore. Have them identify the ways CRS challenges the status quo and calls people to live out a more Christian vision of the world.

Then invite the students to engage in service work related to the topic or country they have chosen. The students can support an international effort by raising funds and contributing them to CRS or by writing letters or making phone calls in support of positive change. Or the students can do a local service project on a similar topic. If they select water quality as an issue, they could link with local efforts to protect a nearby lake or local water supply. If they learn about agricultural practices in Ghana, they could find an issue affecting farmers in their own region. Service projects can be chosen individually, in groups, or as a class.

Close by inviting the students to draw a comparison back to the prophets of the Old Testament. In what ways are the students, CRS staff members, or leaders in local efforts prophets for today's time? How are the responses they encounter similar to the responses met by the Old Testament prophets? How does God inspire those efforts, and in what ways is a spiritually based effort different from a purely secular response?

Service Project Information

Your name: _____

Use this handout to be better informed about the service opportunity you have chosen. Complete the questions before starting your service and return the form to your service coordinator.

1. For what agency are you volunteering?

2. Who is your contact person at the agency? What is the phone number? What is that person's e-mail address?

3. What will your duties be?

4. What times and days are you available to volunteer?

5. What hours, days, or schedule will you have?

6. What is your start date?

7. Is there an application process? Have you completed it?

8. Is there any training required? Have you completed it?

9. What will you be doing for transportation?

(The material in this handout is adapted from *Making the Hours Count: Transforming Your Service Experience Leader's Guide,* by Constance Fourré [Winona, MN: Saint Mary's Press, 2006], pages 18 and 19. Copyright © 2006 by Saint Mary's Press. All rights reserved.)

Service Hours Record

Your Name _____

Agency or Project _____

Date	Hours Served	Description of Activity

(The material in this handout is adapted from *Making the Hours Count: Transforming Your Service Experience Leader's Guide,* by Constance Fourré [Winona, MN: Saint Mary's Press, 2006], pages 18 and 19. Copyright © 2006 by Saint Mary's Press. All rights reserved.)

Chapter 4

Retreats

Overview

Of the various programs within Catholic high school campus ministries, retreats are among the most important and intricate. Well-done retreats can be some of the most effective tools campus ministers use to bring the students to Christ. As such, retreats are foundational to the pastoral life of Catholic high schools.

High school students live in a constant game of tug-of-war, between freedom at one end and dependence on family at the other. Campus ministers can offer acceptance, guidance, and direction to the students during those difficult teen years. Retreats provide a context for ministry to take place on a deeper level for an extended time. Whether the retreats last one afternoon or several days, what can be done with young people during a retreat is far more than can be accomplished during a lunch hour.

Retreats offer the students and adults opportunities to rest, regroup, and realign and spaces to seriously examine their lives in light of the Gospel. Withdrawing from our ordinary and often overscheduled lives to slow down, think, listen, and pray disposes us to the work of the Holy Spirit. All too often, noise, busyness, and a constant state of hurry drown out the tiny, whispering sound of God's unique voice.

Just as a camera must refocus when the view changes, so too the soul needs the time and space to refocus on what matters most. When our bodies and minds begin to slow down, we can more effectively evaluate our priorities. Retreats are great opportunities to explore the cognitive dissonance that occurs when our values and beliefs are out of sync with our actions and lifestyles.

For some, this is a time not only to pray but also to learn about prayer. During those important formative years when young people make many decisions about how they will live, a powerful prayer experience can lead to a lifetime of prayerful dialogue with the living God. The work of retreats is the work of the Holy Spirit. The work of campus ministers is to create an atmosphere where this can happen.

Theology

Solitude in Christ

Although many good reasons exist to take the students on retreats, perhaps the most important is because Jesus went on retreat. The Gospels provide several accounts of Jesus's wandering off in search of solitude for times of prayer (Matt. 14:13, Mark 1:35, Luke 4:42). He modeled for his disciples the necessity of taking extended time away from the demands and distractions of everyday life for prayer and reflection. During these times, he surely heard the voice of his Father (Matt. 3:17, 17:5; Mark 1:11, 9:7; Luke 3:22), reminding him of his core identity, reaffirming his worth, and clarifying his mission and purpose. God desires to do this and more for your students and has the space and time to do it in the context of retreats.

Conversion and Reconciliation

During times of solitude and prayer, the Holy Spirit often moves us to repent, creating opportunities for conversion of our hearts. The New Testament term expressing this concept is *metanoia*. It implies a decision to give our whole lives over to God. Metanoia is more often than not a slow and messy process whereby we choose God daily while stumbling and returning for mercy and forgiveness. Another form of conversion, much more akin to the experiences of Saint Paul and Saint Augustine, is an intense, sudden experience where "scales" fall from our eyes and we see our previous lives in the light of Christ. Although this is a rarer form of conversion, it nonetheless happens among young people, especially on retreats.

Community

One of the primary effects of well-planned retreats is a sense of community that emerges among the staff and retreat participants. Community was an essential element in the life of the early believers (Acts 4:32). Jesus never intended his followers to walk alone. Rather, Christ knew the power of relationships and, as such, built his Church on the power that comes from them. Christ emphasized this when he said, "Where two or three are gathered in my name, I am there in the midst of them" (Matt. 18:20).

When you invite teenagers to risk vulnerability and share from their hearts and receive one another in the same spirit, trust develops, which makes a sense of community possible. Talks, witnesses, journaling, and especially small-group sharing sessions, where affirmation should play a big role—all work together with the Spirit to create an atmosphere of community. Good follow-up work by the retreat team and student leaders reinforces this communal sense in the weeks and months following the retreat and forges strong bonds among the students, who might otherwise remain disconnected and isolated. As more and more young people struggle with wounds of abandonment and broken relationships, the solidarity they can find in Christ may give them the strength to keep going day after day.

Practical Planning Tools

Step One: Objective

Your first step in planning your retreat schedule for the year is deciding what needs the retreats will meet. In general, retreats serve to bring about changes of heart and provide opportunities for deeper reflection and prayer, healing, reconciliation, and class unity. Because these basic needs are present in every high school, beginning here is a good idea. You may wish to add retreats for special occasions, issues, or themes. Those types of thematic retreats can be effective and life giving. Resource 4–A, "Retreat Planning Sheet," provides guidance for planning retreats.

Class Retreats

Class retreats can be extremely powerful experiences of unity for the students. They provide contexts that facilitate building new relationships and strengthening existing bonds that may have slipped away due to the busyness of school life.

Gender Issues

For mixed-gender schools, gender issues can be good reasons not to have typical class retreats. The many differences between adolescent boys and girls often necessitate separation to address specific issues such as sexuality, relationships, bullying and other aggressive behavior, and so on.

Issues and Themes

Specific issues involving grief and tragedy, which occur more often in school life than we would like, are sometimes best handled on retreats. In instances of grief or tragedy, theme-based retreats would be appropriate.

Overnight Retreats

Overnighters are ideal for encouraging the students to delve into deeper issues and allow the ministers and teams the time to minister to the retreat participants through those experiences.

Step Two: Logistics and Budget Issues

Location

Your decision about the location of your retreat will likely combine availability of retreat centers, proximity to your school, and the physical distance retreat participants need to travel to retreat. Because retreat centers fill up quickly, you may need to schedule your retreat dates one or even two years in advance. Most locations require up-front, nonrefundable deposits. Additionally, if your school cannot provide transportation, you will need to estimate the cost of acquiring and using transportation. If possible, it is best not to use volunteers for transportation.

Meeting and Breakout Rooms

Most centers charge à la carte for meeting rooms. Decide in advance the amount of space you need for small-group and large-group gatherings and reserve the space accordingly.

Food

Often, young people's taste in food is drastically simpler and less expensive than adults'. A good rule of thumb is to keep food simple and plentiful. Pizza, hamburgers, and pasta are generally well received. You might need to provide vegetarian options for some of your students. You will also want to find out beforehand if any students have food allergies.

Outdoor Activities

Certain outdoor activities require special equipment or supervision. For example, swimming will require an appropriate number of lifeguards.

Step Three: Schedule

The schedule of a particular retreat should reflect your needs and objectives. If you need to plan a freshman retreat that builds class unity, then your schedule should include lots of time for community building and for sharing. Begin by asking yourself the following questions:
- What time will the retreat begin and end?
- Will the retreat include the Eucharist or the sacrament of Penance and Reconciliation?
- How many meals will be served?
- How many talks are necessary and in what order are they best given?
- Will there be small-group or large-group sharing sessions?
- Is time needed for personal prayer and reflection?

Once you have scheduled your activities, review those objectives and needs. Does this schedule of events meet your needs and objectives? Ask members of your team for input about the schedule. Once you have the talks and other activities mapped out chronologically, assign a time frame to each, making sure to include time for meals and breaks.

Being flexible, yet committed to the retreat schedule, is important. Flexibility allows room for the Spirit to move, and your commitment to the schedule communicates your level of preparation and highlights the significance of the retreat experience.

Step Four: Forms

Release documents protect schools from liability and protect the students in case of medical emergencies. Your school may have a template on file for you to use with the proper legal stipulations. If not, simply create one yourself and submit it to your administrators for approval. These forms have three basic sections: consent, medical release, and registration.

Consent

The purpose of the consent portion of the form is for parents or guardians of the students to give you permission to take their children on the activity by means of an identified mode of transportation. This section should state expectations for any liability parents may incur as a result of the behavior of their children. Include a statement about the enforcement of school policies while on retreat.

Medical Release

The medical release gives you and medical professionals the permission to do what is necessary to protect the students in case of medical emergencies. Provide a place for parents to list any medical conditions their children may have. If retreat participants or youth leaders need medications, it is best to put an adult in charge of distributing them.

Registration

The registration portion contains all pertinent information about the retreat participants and their parents, such as phone numbers and e-mail and mailing addresses, should you need to contact the parents.

Step Five: Team Preparation

Selection

There are myriad factors to consider when selecting retreat teams. The most important is understanding what your team will need to do on retreat. This will influence which youth and adults you select for this ministry.

Training

Training and preparing the team are essential to the success of any retreat. Understand that although many volunteers are well intentioned, they may not have the basic skills to minister among young people in an educational setting. First, assess the skills, maturity, and spirituality of volunteers or other team members, and then provide training that matches the needs of the team.

This training can be as simple as a meeting with the retreat staff a week or a few days before the retreat. It can be as elaborate as a couple of meetings combined with a handbook of expectations and defined staff roles. You must judge the type of training that will work best. Begin by asking yourself the following questions: "What am I training them for?" "What do I need them to do?" These two questions should guide how you train your team.

Because teamwork is essential for retreat teams, consider using icebreakers and other team-building activities that build trust and community. These will help your members perform as a team rather than a group of individuals. If your team members are not comfortable around one another, then the retreat participants likely will pick up on this vibe and not feel comfortable either.

No matter how old or experienced the group serving on the retreat is, remind them of the basic expectations of leadership. Urge them to see themselves as leaders and take ownership of the retreat. As the director, you want *them* to notice if something is not going right. Resource 4–B, "Preparing Your Retreat Team and Small-Group Leaders," offers ideas on choosing and readying your core group of retreat leaders.

Talks

Talks are one of the principal venues to articulate the content of your objectives. The talks need to have a good balance of content and testimony. Avoid having too much of either in any one talk. A content-rich talk, no matter how eloquent, will create the feeling of a classroom. Similarly, a testimony with no message lacks purpose and has no connection to your objectives. Ideally, strike a balance between the two so the message or theme is communicated within the context of a person's life story. Achieving this balance requires a conscious effort on your part and that of your retreat team. Resource 4–C, "Talk Tips," gives advice on achieving that balance. It is also important for you to know what is going to be said in each talk. Keep in mind what is an appropriate level of sharing in talks. By listening to all talks before a retreat and having the speakers write down their intended messages, you can ensure that inappropriate or deeply personal material is not shared. This applies for talks given by youth and adults.

Activities

In addition to talks, activities are integral parts of most retreats. Activities related to the themes presented in the talks invite the participants to enter the topic more actively. On any retreat, offer a variety of activities ranging from icebreakers and other physical activities to quiet reflection, journaling, and other quiet activities. By using a variety of senses and experiences, you engage more students in participating in the retreat. Activities, like all other aspects of a retreat, must be planned in advance, have a distinct purpose, and work to promote the topics of the retreat. Through integrating talks, activities, discussions, and prayers, you can construct a retreat that achieves the desired goals.

Step Six: Confidentiality and Pastoral Care

Pastoral care of young people is one of the most complex areas of campus ministries. Although some direction exists concerning pastoral care of young people, the specific issue of confidentiality still remains vague, and consequently precarious, for campus ministers, especially in retreat settings.

At one time it was common to hear the phrase "What is shared on a retreat stays on the retreat." Today, campus ministers serve in settings overshadowed by legal and safety issues that require extra vigilance. The ministry of Catholic high schools exists within a larger ministry of the Church to Catholic families. Although your primary responsibility is to your students, the challenge is to remember that the students are members of families, and their parents have a right to know certain information regarding their children's well-being. In cases of abuse or physical harm to oneself or another person, adults and student ministers are legally bound to report such cases to the proper authorities.

Campus ministers should notify the students and adults at the beginning of a retreat of the specific terms of confidentiality. Although it is still a good idea to set the expectation of general confidentiality over the context of the entire retreat to create a safe atmosphere for the students to share freely, you cannot promise unbreakable confidentiality. Your school's counseling department can be a great resource in helping sift through some of these complicated issues. Also consult your diocesan office about diocesan policies on confidentiality, chaperone guidelines, and required training for volunteers working with young people.

Step Seven: Reentry and Follow-Up

After retreats or similarly powerful spiritual experiences, young people often experience "retreat highs," heightened emotional and spiritual states. Those experiences can be especially powerful for anyone, especially teenagers, many of whom are having their first tangible experiences of God. When the emotions inevitably begin to subside, the students might wonder what happened to God. This can be very disappointing and cause some to dismiss their experiences of God as illusions. This is when they need support the most. It is essential that members of the retreat, preferably adults or team members who connected with the individuals on retreat, are there to support the retreat participants as they reenter the "real world," reassuring them of the reality of their God experiences while on retreat, despite what they feel later. The presence of a loving, accepting, and reassuring familiar face will serve to validate their retreat experiences, giving God's grace opportunities to soak more deeply into the participants' hearts.

One effective way to help the students reenter is to plan follow-up sessions. These can take the form of large-group gatherings over a meal or simply gatherings of the small groups from the retreat just to touch base and see how the group members are doing. Retreat participants need a safe place to process their experiences of reentry. Parents and peers often struggle with accepting the changes that take place in the participants while on retreat. Good follow-up not only gives the students an opportunity to vent but also can be used to give them tips on how to effectively communicate their retreat experiences to their parents and friends.

While still on retreat, it is helpful to discuss with the students some of the issues and challenges they will face upon returning home. Being honest with teens concerning the inevitable climb down from the mountaintop will help them face the challenges of reentry.

You will also want to provide opportunities for retreat evaluation by the retreat participants, retreat team, and adult volunteers. For the retreat participants and adult volunteers, simple questionnaires about what they liked, disliked, and will take away from the retreat and suggestions for future retreats will provide you with useful feedback. For the retreat team, you might consider an evaluation meeting to discuss the retreat process from planning through follow-up. This is another chance to gather useful information for future retreats and to acknowledge what the team did well.

Conclusion

Although retreats require much planning and effort from you and your team, they can profoundly affect the retreat participants and adults. For the participants, retreats may be the most memorable and enriching experiences of their high school lives. Retreat ministry can lead team members to continued ministry in the Church long after high school has ended.

Schools benefit immeasurably from good retreat programs. When the students come back to school after retreats, the Spirit, which is fresh and alive in them, spreads to others. This positively affects all areas of school life, especially the other areas of your ministry programs. Remember that retreat ministry is a process. Your commitment to the process of training your teams and journeying with those attending the retreats will bear much fruit.

Retreat Planning Sheet

I. Needs and objectives

List the needs this retreat is meeting for your school community and your objectives for the retreat.

The reason we are having this retreat is (class unity, seasonal, service, and so on): _____
_____
_____
_____.

I would like our students to leave the retreat having experienced: _____
_____
_____
_____.

I would like our students to leave the retreat knowing: _____
_____
_____
_____.

I would like our students to leave the retreat feeling: _____
_____
_____
_____.

I would like our students to leave the retreat believing: _____
_____
_____
_____.

I would like our students to leave the retreat committed to: _____
_____
_____
_____.

I would like our students to leave the retreat having heard: _____

_____

_____

_____

_____ .

I would like our students to leave the retreat [add your own]: _____

_____

_____

_____

_____ .

II. Budget

Total the per-participant cost of your retreat by estimating the cost of each item below:

Facility Usage Total $_____

Transportation Costs $_____ (large group)

                                         $_____ (team and leaders)

Supplies $_____

Budgetary Offset or Other $_____ (if applicable)

Total Retreat Cost $_____

Divide by Number of

Paying Participants   _____ = $_____ per participant

Preparing Your Retreat Team and Small-Group Leaders

Selecting a Team

One of your first responsibilities is to develop a retreat team. You will benefit from having a team of students, faculty or staff members, and parents to plan and implement the retreat. If retreat teams or campus ministry teams already exist, use them and add other members of your community who will be helpful to the retreat process. The number of team members is up to you. A good rule to follow is one team member for every six to eight participants. You also may want to consider having enough team members to have one student team member and one adult team member join each small group.

Student Team Members

In selecting students to be on the team, consider the following questions:
- Are the students mature enough to lead their classmates?
- Do the students reflect the morals and faith you are calling the retreat participants to?
- Do the students represent a cross section of the student body?
- Do the students bring a variety of talents and gifts to the team?
- Do the students include both those who are comfortable in front of people and those who prefer behind-the-scenes work? In other words, are both introverts and extroverts on the team?

In selecting the students for the team, be aware of the variety of tasks required for the retreat. Some students who appear to be obvious choices may not be the best students for the team. Remember that you need students who will be comfortable, and thrive, in doing tasks that the retreat participants might not notice. The selection of team members will convey a strong message to the class about their inclusion or exclusion on the retreat. By inviting a diverse group of students to join the team, you send the idea that the retreat is truly for all participants.

Adult Team Members

Include adult team members who have experience with retreats and are familiar with the students. In terms of faculty and staff members, this means inviting teachers who not only teach but also are involved in extracurricular activities. Ask yourself the same questions you did in selecting the students for the team. In particular, have you invited teachers and staff members whom different groups of students can identify with and who have a variety of gifts and talents?

Parents are a little trickier. Before you invite parents, ask their students attending the retreat if they are okay with the parents' attendance. Consider inviting parents of the students who are not attending the retreat.

Preparing the Team

Begin by letting your team members know they may be asked to do some or all of the following:

- meet several times to prepare for the retreat
- lead small groups
- give talks during the retreat
- actively participate in all activities
- give directions for activities
- plan and lead prayer experiences
- plan and prepare the retreat environment

Ideally, the team members share the responsibility for all tasks, but this is not always possible. If some team members are new to retreats, ask them to handle less-demanding tasks.

Hold several team planning meetings to prepare for the retreat. Start each meeting with a prayer, asking different members to prepare the prayer each time.

If your diocese offers a youth leadership program, encourage the student team members to attend. Many skills taught in such programs—communication, group dynamics, listening, goal setting, and so on—can be helpful for the retreat.

Emphasize that team members are also retreat participants. All team members—including the adults—are required to participate in all activities. You cannot expect the student participants to work together and participate actively when team members sit out some activities.

Preparing for Small Groups

Small-group times can be essential elements of any retreat. With this in mind, you and your team must devote time to setting up the small groups for success. You can do the following things to this end:

- **Form the small groups before the retreat.** Decide in advance which students will be in which groups.
- **In forming the groups, be aware of cliques and conflicts within the student community.** Include a few of your student team members in forming small groups. They will help you form groups that are not dominated by one group of friends and that do not have students with major personality conflicts.
- **Keep small groups to a manageable number.** Allow fewer than ten students, and preferably six to eight.
- **Allow the student team members to select which small groups and which adults they will work with, when possible.** Again, the goal is to establish harmonious small groups. Letting team members have a say in the group selection helps avoid potential conflicts. This also applies to adult team members in the small groups.

- **Be aware of existing adult-student conflicts.** Before placing teachers or other adults in small groups, review the groups with the adults to ensure the adults have positive relationships with all the students.

Getting Started with Your Small Groups

Once the retreat has started, you face the challenge of getting the students into their small groups and starting the sharing. In several different ways, such as the following, you can have the students identify which small groups they are in:

- **Have the small-group leaders make name tags unique to their small groups.** For example, one group might have name tags that are crosses with the students' names written on them. When the time comes to get in small groups for the first time, have the students find everyone with the same name tags. If you go this route, have each small-group leader make several extra name tags in case someone was overlooked or needs to change groups for some reason.
- **Place a specific designating mark such as a letter or number on each generic name tag.** Again, when it is time to get in small groups for the first time, have participants find everyone with the same designations.
- **Post small-group lists on the walls in the meeting rooms along with designated gathering areas.** Have the students find which groups they are in and go to their designated areas.
- **Form small groups from people who share cabins or rooms.** This helps conversations continue during unstructured time. The downside is that this limits student contact with others on the retreat.

When small groups meet for the first time, the members should introduce themselves. Also, lay ground rules for the groups. These include the following:

- **Respect other members both in and out of the small-group meetings.** This means listening when someone is sharing and respectfully addressing other group members.
- **The small groups are places for honest sharing.** Acknowledge your own confidentiality (share what you are comfortable sharing). Ask groups not to share with others outside their groups anything group members share in the group.
- **Be willing to seek outside advice.** If topics come up that you are uncomfortable with or need to discuss with someone outside the groups, contact the retreat director or another adult.

(The material in this resource is adapted from *The Covenant Retreat: A Discernment Experience for High School Seniors,* edited by Steven C. McGlaun et al. [Winona, MN: Saint Mary's Press, 2005], pages 88–91. Copyright © 2005 by Saint Mary's Press. All rights reserved.)

Talk Tips

A talk, or sharing, occurs during each session of a retreat. Often, there are two talks—one given by a student and another by an adult. They are important parts of the retreat and can have a tremendous effect when done correctly. When preparing the students and adults to give talks, stress the following key points:

- **No talks should exceed five minutes.** This "rule of five" is extremely important to keep the attention of the participants.

- **No speakers should just wing their talks.** All talks need to be written out, rehearsed, and shared with you before they are delivered. The speakers should not read from their sheets. Writing the talks out beforehand, however, clarifies the talks in the speakers' minds and acts as a resource if the speakers get off topic or forget what they were going to say.

- **Balance heartfelt sharing with confidentiality.** Nothing should be shared that would embarrass the speakers or anyone else. Any sharing that involves family or friends should be cleared with those people before the talks. For adults, this is equally important. Nothing should be shared that will negatively affect the adults' roles in their communities.

- **Before the retreat, work extensively with the people giving talks.** This includes praying with, offering feedback to, and assisting the speakers with public-speaking skills.

- **Be present at all talks on the retreat.** Ahead of time, work out signals with the speakers to offer direction and support during the talks. These can include signals to offer encouragement, get back on track when off topic, and wrap up when the talks run long. Intervene if the speakers are severely off track or sharing inappropriate material.

(The material in this handout is adapted from *The Covenant Retreat: A Discernment Experience for High School Seniors,* edited by Steven C. McGlaun et al. [Winona, MN: Saint Mary's Press, 2005], page 98. Copyright © 2005 by Saint Mary's Press. All rights reserved.)

Chapter 5

Leadership Development

Overview

You are looking for the students to take the lead. In addition to leaders for prayers, retreats, and service experiences, you are looking for role models for high school youth trying to navigate their way through adolescence. The good news for campus ministers is that God has provided all the leadership gifts Catholic high schools require. There are plenty of gifted prayer leaders, creative retreat planners, and students who choose to be dedicated to community service. As a campus minister, you have the particular privilege of discovering, forming, and empowering those student leaders. Together, you and your student leaders can enable your school community to express its connection to God in ways that make sense. In addition, you are in a unique position to set the stage for a lifetime of leading and learning.

As you look out at a sea of new faces at the start of a school year and realize that the seniors you had come to depend on are no longer in the audience, you may feel you are starting all over again. Remember that campus ministers establish a certain rhythm—a cycle of discovery, formation, and empowerment. That cycle begins when you meet the wide-eyed freshmen, and it continues until you open wide the school doors and send your graduates out into the world to serve as Jesus served. Long before they are ready to explore leadership roles, your students will pay attention to how leaders look, what they do, and how the community values their service.

Schools are naturally oriented toward the future—as is our Church. In our schools and in our Church, we are committed to transforming the present, because we believe it will make a difference—not only in our schools but also in our families, our churches, and ultimately in the world. Lay leaders (and that is precisely what your student leaders are) are found "in each and in all of the secular professions and occupations. They live in the ordinary circumstances of family and social life, from which the very web of their existence is woven. They are called there by God that . . . they may work for the sanctification of the world from within" (*Lumen Gentium*, no. 31). When you look to discover leaders, be sure you are looking in all the corners of your school. Potential pastoral leaders can be found leading as your school's class officers, marching in a band, running on the track, sketching in a corner of the art studio, or curling up against the lockers plugged into a music player. You are searching for all varieties of students, because your ministry is charged with reaching all varieties. I often tell parents of incoming freshmen that we are not expecting that they are sending us leaders. Instead, I say we will spend the next four years helping their children appreciate and practice using their gifts and learn how to transfer their school experiences to leadership in the world. That is the incredible idea the Second Vatican Council shared with us: God calls ordinary people to build the Kingdom right where they are. You have an extraordinary opportunity to help young people learn how to do that.

Campus ministers point out specific ways individual students can make a difference. You understand that ministerial leadership is built on giftedness, and so you pay attention to discovering, forming, and empowering those gifts. It is what Jesus did. He noticed people in the crowd, invited them to follow, encouraged them to pay attention to the experiences they were having together, and then sent them out to build the Kingdom. If we depend on Jesus's model and believe we can recognize God's presence by paying attention, campus ministers will develop leaders by inviting them to learn how to pay attention to God.

Theology

"Community is God's promise to those who have accepted the gracious invitation to live the gospel and to be lights for the world" (USCCB, Secretariat for Family, Laity, Women, and Youth, "A Vision of Faith for Young Adults"). Leaders in our churches and in our schools are empowered to be community builders so they can ultimately be Kingdom builders. Early in Mark's Gospel, we hear the challenging reminder that "the time is fulfilled, and the Kingdom of God has come near" (1:15). Clearly, our Church and the Scriptures suggest that if the Gospel is to enlighten the world, and if we are to recognize the promise of the Kingdom, we will look to real, live sons and daughters of God to point the way. That is precisely why we form leaders in our schools. We want to be certain that when teens look across the aisle in a classroom, encounter classmates in the cafeteria line, train in the gym, practice for the school play, or gather with friends on Saturday night, they are engaged with someone who has decided to share in Jesus's mission to build the Kingdom.

For Catholics, our theology of Kingdom building and our approach to engaging our communities in the action of building the Kingdom experienced a significant shift with the Second Vatican Council. Although the council may seem like ancient history to our student leaders, the *Pastoral Constitution on the Church in the Modern World (Gaudium et Spes, 1965)* provided a new lens for examining our relationships to the world we hope to transform. That lens continues to demand that we as the Church (and the church that is a Catholic high school) must be communities living in the heart of the world to minister to it. In other words, the world sets the agenda for the Church and our school. Although we campus ministers hold powerful places in the lives of young people as role models and mentors, we do not live in the heart of the world of the teens we serve— we are no longer high school students. We do, however, have the privilege and opportunity to form young leaders who are firmly planted in the adventure called adolescence. Can we form them into Kingdom builders?

Building the Kingdom of God may sound like an overwhelming addition to a campus minister's job description. Can you trust the mission of the Church to a bunch of high school students? It might be easier just to do all the jobs yourself. Discovering, forming, and empowering leaders is messy, takes time, and never turns out the same way twice. It requires a certain amount of risk taking: do you really believe the Kingdom is being built in your school? On those days when you wonder if all the messiness is worth it, remember that each of us has already been called and gifted in Baptism. Because of Baptism, every Christian is called to be a contributing member of the Body of Christ. Are you ready to cooperate with baptismal grace? As a campus minister, you have the chance to claim the promises of Baptism and to call leaders to discipleship—one by one. Jesus did it precisely that way: he invited ordinary people; he let people walk beside him, watch, and listen; he encouraged tough questions; he always stuck around to see his followers through to the answers; and finally, he sent them out to change the world. When we discover, form, and empower the gifts for our schools, we look toward the future. We are building our Church and building our world—we are building the Kingdom. That makes all the messiness worthwhile.

Practical Planning Tools

Discovering Leaders

Vision Matters

It sounds simple, but you will never discover leaders if they do not know what you do. Your ability to articulate a clear vision for every component of campus ministry is essential. Not only does a clear vision help potential leaders know what they are becoming involved in, it also assures them you have a clear idea of where you are going. Jesus attracted followers because they trusted he had a plan: Peter and Andrew dropped their nets; James and John left their boat; Zacchaeus climbed out of a tree. Pay consistent attention to the ways you can communicate your vision. As a campus minister, you have the privilege of opening the possibility of the students leading each other to experiences of God in one another.

Use Community Prayer

The single most effective way to communicate the vision of your campus ministry program is through daily community prayer. Well-crafted prayers announce the presence of God in words your community understands and connects the real world your students live in to a real God. Do not underestimate those opportunities to develop a Catholic identity your leaders can articulate. Each time we deliberately pray together, we respond to a rhythm that is countercultural: we are stopping, pausing, and taking a breath. We admit we are somehow connected to the Divine Mystery, we are part of a family that is even bigger than our school, and our bodies, minds, and hearts are practicing how to tap into a language that will speak to us for the rest of our lives. *Lex orandi, lex credendi*—"how we pray is how we believe." Your leaders—and potential leaders—need this language. Use the public address system to pray together at the start of each day. It may be the most important few minutes of your school day.

Communicate Leadership Opportunities

Most schools have a system for daily communication. Be sure campus ministry activities and needs are included. This practice reinforces campus ministry activities as part of the regular rhythm of your school. When the school community is accustomed to hearing about campus ministry, its members assume it makes a vital contribution to the institution. In addition, that communication affirms the students who are already part of leadership teams and plants the seeds of possibilities in the hearts and minds of the students who are waiting to be discovered as leaders.

Rely on the Scripture's Advice

"Ask, and it will be given you; search, and you will find; knock, and the door will be opened for you" (Luke 11:9). Let your community know about the leaders you need. Use a time and talent volunteer sign-up at the start of the school year. Yearly stewardship sign-ups are common in parishes, so for many of your students, it is a familiar practice. Visit every theology classroom during the first week of school. Offer a sign-up form that includes every imaginable job—from reading at Mass to handing out worship aids at the door before services. Explain the leadership roles available, the time commitment each involves, and the training that will be provided to assist students in their ministries. The time and talent sign-up should be clear that there are many different gifts and that there is room for everyone. Share that not every ministry is a good fit for every person. Certain ministries, such as lectoring or leading small groups, require additional discernment by the volunteers and campus ministers. If you ask for help, be sure to use those who volunteer. It is tempting to ask the same tried-and-true students. That, however, leaves little room for discovering, forming, and empowering anyone new. Resource 5–A, "Student Volunteer Form (Sample)," offers examples of what you might include to gather potential leaders.

Formation for Leadership

Model Leadership in Your Ministry

When the student leaders encounter you, they must receive a living lesson in servant leadership, an example of how it looks to serve as Jesus served. Are you prepared to say, "This is what loving God looks like"? Jesus's message was consistent and attractive; it called people to wholeness. Catholicism expresses its uniqueness in describing itself as a sacramental Church: an outward sign to the entire world of the truth, service, and communion for those who choose to model their lives on Christ. Campus ministers face the challenge of being outward signs of that consistent and attractive message to build something new—in our schools and in the world. We get the chance to accompany teens enmeshed in, entangled by, and entranced with the business of growing up. In our campus ministry offices, we gather under the umbrella of God, and we greet one another, listen, ask forgiveness, extend pardon, say thank you, eat together, sing together, plan together, and explore the possibilities of life, Church, and faith.

Our student leaders are watching us: how does loving God on an ordinary day really look? In practical ways, what does it look like to pay attention in a way Jesus might? The simple action of putting down your pen when a student approaches your desk can send a dynamic message: "What you need to say to me is important," and "People are always more important than things."

It Is a 14-Inch Drop from the Head to the Heart

The translation of faith from intellectual musings to a radical falling in love with God and a decision to serve God's people depends on whether our students are led to experiences of conversion that call them into covenant with God. Although the notion of conversion has been comfortably couched in discussions of entering the Roman Catholic Tradition or simply turning away from sin, the experience of conversion is not neatly tucked away in compartments labeled *Catholic, sin,* or *Sunday.* Part of the challenge and privilege of campus ministry is accompanying leaders as they learn to articulate what God has to do with life.

Engaging the students in theological reflections can set into motion this process of connecting God with experiences. One way to make that connection is through the use of reflection questions. Such questions, which provoke reflection and encourage theological connections, enable our leaders to claim their own experiences of God and then share those lived experiences with their larger communities. For example, ask the following questions:

- When were you most aware of God's presence today?
- What does holiness look like?
- Where do you find support in trying to make good decisions?
- We are familiar with the Gospel stories of lepers and Samaritans. Who are the "lepers" and "Samaritans" in our school?

Providing opportunities for our student leaders to reflect theologically gives a model of attention to the difference God's presence makes in our experiences.

Leaders Are Important

Be intentional about communicating the value of leaders and the contributions they can make to the school. When gathering a leadership team that will work together for an entire school year, you begin to articulate their potential contributions by describing team members and carefully outlining their responsibilities. Resource 5–B, "Peer Ministry Team Job Description (Sample)," gives potential leaders an idea of what to expect as members of the campus ministry team. The questions on resource 5–C, "Peer Ministry or Campus Ministry Team Application (Sample)," will help campus ministers recognize future leaders. Clear communication at this juncture is essential. In addition, an application process (rather than casual invitations to the students you think may be interested) underscores the value your school places on the commitment you are inviting. The process also communicates that every student is a potential leader and is invited to consider completing an application.

In addition to articulating clear team descriptions and outlining responsibilities, you can in many other ways recognize the contributions of the student leaders and prepare them for leadership positions. Provide the student leaders with binders they bring to meetings and carry to class. In them, they can keep calendars, agendas, and important information about the projects with which they are involved. Binders with see-through covers are ideal. They make it easy for everyone to see that the student leaders are carrying, for example, a "KAIROS Retreat Team" binder or the official binder of the "Christmas Adopt-a-Family Chairperson." Being organized in this way helps student leaders better fulfill their commitments.

Leaders also appreciate having tangible items that identify them as significant students in the school community. T-shirts are popular among student leaders as concrete ways to proclaim their important roles in the school. Think about ways you can direct attention to your leaders. Remember, these are the young people you are encouraging others to follow.

Plan to Develop Leadership Skills

The student leaders are learning to lead and will depend on you to teach them what they need to know. When forming a peer ministry team, for example, be sure that developing leadership skills is part of your meeting schedules. In addition to planning retreats and participating in special events, leadership team members must take time to cultivate the skills they will need to serve the community as leaders. When planning your yearly calendar for a leadership team, include sessions that provide opportunities to practice the following skills:

Active listening skills
- Decide to listen.
- Look at the speaker.
- Let your body posture say "You have my undivided attention."
- Think about what you are hearing—what is the main idea?
- Ask questions.
- Do not assume you know what the speaker is going to say—be ready to be surprised!
- Respond positively—affirm the speaker.

- Tell the speaker what you think you heard him or her say—summarize and ask if you are correct.
- Do not give advice or solve problems—just listen.
- Observe active listeners.

Public speaking skills

Guidelines for writing a retreat or witness talk (See chapter 4 for tips on giving talks.)

Empowering Leaders

Group Goals Contribute to Success

Provide ways for leaders to think together. Brainstorming sessions enable everyone's ideas to be heard; all ideas are recorded and considered when brainstorming. A simple way to facilitate collecting as many ideas as possible is to designate a "planning wall." Taping newsprint to a wall and providing plenty of colored markers encourages your leaders to record every idea. The planning wall is a living document: the students can wander in at any time and add ideas or pose questions for the group to consider; the sheets of paper can easily be rearranged. When you finally decide which pieces of the plan to implement, you can be sure the entire group has owned the process, because you created the living document together.

Be Willing to Have Tough Conversations

Adults who minister to teens are well served when they reflect on the following relationship question: are you willing to be a mentor to your leaders? Committed to the growth of the students whom you mentor you must be willing to be the voice that compels the student leaders to examine how their lives reflect their status as role models. Although being friendly and approachable is important, remember that you are an adult, not a peer of your student leaders. Your responsibility is to hold the student leaders accountable for their commitment to academics, as well as their commitment to campus ministry leadership; for their actions on weekends, as well as their actions on retreats. If you suspect you are mentoring leaders who are making poor decisions regarding drugs, alcohol, or sexual activity, your responsibility as a ministry mentor is to model care-filled confrontation. If members of your leadership team are struggling with respectful relationships with other team members, it is up to you to initiate a process that models how people communicate needs and concerns to one another. We get a glimpse of caring confrontation as the Gospel of John describes the beginning of Jesus's public ministry. Jesus was not afraid to ask a jolting question at the wedding at Cana. Jesus's response to his mother surprises the reader: "Woman, what concern is that to you and to me?" (2:4). John's Gospel encourages readers to examine what Jesus's revelation of the Father may actually have to do with them. Jesus's question begins to move readers step by step through the relentless challenge of examining the ultimate questions, such as, do we or do we not reveal the God who is love? Likewise, do your student leaders, in their ordinary lives, reveal the God who is love?

"I Thank My God Every Time I Remember You . . ." (Phil. 1:3)

Always remember to say thank you. When your leaders have completed a project, ministered at prayer, or assisted with a school event, model gratitude by taping a thank-you note to their lockers or in another way.

Let Your Leaders Lead

The reason we spend time discovering and forming leaders is so we can give them the tools they need to step out and minister to their peers. When it is time for the Eucharistic celebration to begin, for a retreat to get started, or for a project to be launched, the most difficult part of your job is done. You have identified gifts, articulated expectations, provided clear instructions, and facilitated group goal setting. Allow your leaders to learn by actually leading. This is the messy part. It is possible not everything will go according to the original plan. That possibility provides your leaders with important life lessons: flexibility, teamwork, and the importance of evaluation.

Evaluate to Help Leaders Grow

When an event is completed, provide time for feedback and evaluation by your leaders. Use the opportunity to take participants and leaders through a process of theological reflection. Following a retreat, for example, you might ask the participants what they heard the speakers say about how God works in their lives. The leaders could reflect on what they discovered about God in the process of facilitating the retreat. Sharing faith takes us out of our heads and into our hearts. It highlights the reality that we all have a share in building the Kingdom of God.

Conclusion

Campus ministry in Catholic high schools is an extraordinary challenge and a significant privilege. What we do involves teaching about, as well as living, faith. We are companions of young men and women who are filled with questions and who wonder if questioning means that they are growing or that they are unbelievers. Our students are curious about how the Catholic religious Tradition creates space for the questions in their lives. And on particularly daring days, they wonder: can one person really change the world—can I really build the Kingdom of God? On those daring days, our Church hopes the students encounter campus ministers who believe and model that the Word not only once became flesh, but the Word is still becoming flesh in us. We campus ministers find ourselves in privileged positions: we are committed to be companions of young people as they struggle with tough questions and ask themselves what loving God means and how to love God as Catholics. The questions are not typical, consistent, or predictable. They require attention and a willingness to listen in unscheduled ways. We are not inviting the student leaders to theoretical activities or to an acceptance of a series of propositions but rather to activities of the heart that have the potential to form the fabric of the life of our schools. Perhaps, together, we will discover that the answer is still the Word.

Student Volunteer Form (Sample)

Whenever you ask for volunteers, get the information you need to help you contact them. Specific information about class schedules and locker numbers makes communication easier. Also be clear that some volunteer opportunities require extra training.

Name: **Locker Number:**

Grade (circle one):   9   10   11   12

Theology teacher/hour, first semester:
Theology teacher/hour, second semester:
Study hall, first semester:
Study hall, second semester:

Time and Talent:

I would like to share my time and talent in the ministries below. I understand that some training or practice may be required.

___ Small-group leader during Advent and Lent lunchtime discussions (one after-school training session; all discussion materials are provided)

___ Lector (proclaims the Scriptures or other readings at liturgies and prayer services)

___ Liturgy coordinator (helps plan liturgies and prayer services, prepares the auditorium for Mass, checks that all ministers have checked in and have everything needed)
Music:

   Your instrument: _____

   Solo_____

   With a group _____

___ Cantor, song leader, or participant in music ensemble for Mass

___ Greeter or usher (greets those attending prayer services, distributes music or other worship aids, ushers during Communion)

___ Altar server

   ___ I am a server.

   ___ I want to be trained as a server.

___ Daily prayer leader (prepares and leads daily prayers with the school community at the beginning of the day—campus minister provides a rubric and assists with the preparation)

___ Main office greeter (The students at all grade levels may serve as greeters at the main entrance to school during study hall—open the door for visitors and direct them to the office. The students are typically assigned for one week a semester. The office secretary will contact you with your assignment.)

Peer Ministry Team
Job Description (Sample)

The first page of an application packet for student leadership might include the following descriptions of team members and their responsibilities.

Members of the peer ministry team may have the following characteristics:
- love God and are comfortable talking about their faith and commitment to Christ
- are leaders in our school and in their families, churches, and communities
- understand that leaders are expected to lead by example every day—on and off campus (yes, that includes weekends and spring break!)
- have earned the respect of their peers, as well as of the faculty and staff members
- have the time to commit themselves to this responsibility
- are known for keeping commitments and honoring deadlines
- have a quarterly C average or above in every class

The peer ministry team members are responsible for some, but not necessarily all, of the following:
- attending a two-day, overnight leadership retreat on the following dates: August 8 and 9
- meeting weekly for leadership training and retreat planning: Tuesdays after school, 2:50 p.m.–3:30 p.m.
- facilitating freshman orientation on the following date: August 24
- organizing Back-to-School Night
- planning and presenting "Celebrate Seniors Morning"—September 8
- planning and presenting a one-day retreat for ninth graders—October 14
- leading an evening eighth-grade event—October 21
- open house—November 14
- planning and presenting a one-day retreat for juniors—January 6
- planning and presenting a one-day retreat for sophomores—March 11
- participating in Advent and Lent lunchtime discussion groups
- planning and presenting "Secret Senior Overnight"—April 7
- participating in liturgies and prayer services

Peer Ministry or Campus Ministry Team Application (Sample)

1. Why do you wish to be involved with peer ministry or campus ministry?

2. What are your interests in the following areas of peer ministry or campus ministry (rank 1, 2, 3, with 1 indicating most interested)

   _____ retreat ministry _____ liturgical ministry _____outreach or service ministry

3. What are your gifts, strengths, or leadership qualities?

4. In which areas of your life do you need to grow to become the person you want to be?

5. To which groups, clubs, or teams do you belong, both in school and in the community?

6. Do you attend church? How often? To which church do you belong? Are you involved in the church youth program?

7. Describe your involvement with your church.

8. What does the term *ministry* mean to you? List words you believe characterize effective ministry.

9. How can the peer ministry or campus ministry team help our students build a stronger faith community? (Be specific.)

10. What do you see as the role of the peer ministry or campus ministry team at our school?

11. What do you believe are the biggest challenges facing the students at our school today?

12. Does your schedule allow for four to eight hours per month for meetings and activities and for spiritual and ministry formation? How do you intend to create a healthy balance with other commitments?

13. A member of the peer ministry or campus ministry team is expected to live and share the Gospel. How would someone describe evidence of this characteristic in you?

Chapter 6

Spirituality and the Daily Life of the Minister

Overview

Ministry in Catholic school settings can be stressful, frustrating, exhilarating, and personally enriching. In the same day, it is possible to experience the most rewarding and challenging moments of your career. With all their ups and downs, twists and turns, campus ministries are a lot like roller coaster rides, delivering unexpected surprises at every turn. Your ministry will call on all the emotional and spiritual resources you possess and will challenge you to acquire even more.

As more and more of the lay faithful accept positions in school ministries, they must have the wherewithal to draw energy and creativity from their ongoing relationships with God. For laity who do not necessarily benefit from the structures or rules of life that religious orders provide, it is vital to proactively develop and sustain a personal spirituality compatible with the pastoral demands of the contemporary world.

To this end, you may find it helpful to associate yourself with particular spiritual "schools," or disciplines, such as those rooted in various religious orders, whose founders' charisms are evidenced by the way their members live out their vocations. Before adopting for yourself a spirituality that works for someone else, be sure to take inventory of the aspects of your personality. This will serve as a guide to help you discern which of the many spiritual models is best suited for you. Most important is that you recognize the necessity of purposefully developing and nurturing your own spiritual life and not relying on someone else to do it for you.

Personal Prayer Life

During the school day, you are called on to be a listening ear, wise counselor, motivator, cheerleader, and mentor. Staying centered as you move among these many roles can be challenging. In prayer, God gives meaning to the endless string of seemingly disconnected experiences in ministry. In the context of prayerful reflection, you will see with greater clarity the purpose and direction of your life and ministry.

In addition to helping you be more centered and grounded, your time in prayer will begin to expose areas in your life that are broken and in need of healing. Your ability to accept those areas that have been in darkness and expose them to the healing light of God's love will be one of the greatest gifts you can bring into your ministry. When we can accept and love the sins, hurts, and brokenness in our hearts, we can offer the same acceptance and love to those in our school community. This gift of compassion is hard, Henri Nouwen writes,

> because it requires the inner disposition to go with others to the place where they are weak, vulnerable, lonely, and broken. But this is not our spontaneous response to suffering. What we desire most is to do away with suffering by fleeing from it or finding a quick cure for it. As busy, active, relevant ministers, we want to earn our bread by making a real contribution. This means first and foremost doing something to show that our presence makes a difference. And so we ignore our greatest gift, which is our ability to enter into solidarity with those who suffer. (*The Way of the Heart*, p. 20)

Some people avoid prayer because of fear. Entering the presence of God makes us vulnerable. Getting out of the driver's seat and giving the steering wheel to God is difficult for those of us used to being in roles of leadership. It is only natural that as we take the roles of passengers, we experience some uneasiness and resistance. Our minds, which are used to being active, functional, and efficient, need time to adjust to the slower pace of prayer, which is different from our everyday lives, where deadlines, results, and accuracy are paramount. Meeting God in prayer has less to do with efficiency and results and more to do with being in relationship.

The beginning stages of this process of surrender will be slow and difficult. We may seem to make little, if any, progress. Remember that prayer is a relationship, and as in any other relationship, our participation, along with God's, is always about the exchange of love rather than reciprocation of favors. Not being discouraged is important during these early days. The goal of prayer is not any particular result; rather, it has much more to do with being faithful to the discipline and the process.

One of the firstfruits of prayer is seeing God more clearly in those you serve. As this begins to happen, the activities of your ministry will emerge from a sense of compassion and empathy rather than obligation. This new way of seeing, this purity of heart, Henri Nouwen says,

> allows us to see more clearly, not only our own needy, distorted, and anxious self but also the caring face of our compassionate God. When that vision remains clear and sharp, it will be possible to move into the midst of a tumultuous world with a heart at rest. It is this restful heart that will attract those who are groping to find their way through life. When we have found our rest in God we can do nothing other than minister. (*The Way of the Heart*, pp. 72–73)

Possessing a discipline for their spiritual lives is important for ministers. Nothing worthwhile is accomplished without discipline. It takes our thoughts and feelings out of the equation and enables us to live in the power of our habits. If we can develop the disciplines of prayer and spirituality, we will then be able to reap the fruits that come from them.

Location

A natural place for prayer may be your school's chapel. If praying in the place where you do ministry muddies the waters of your prayer, find a local church or a prayer chapel. Some find that praying in their homes works best. If you can find a place in your home that is free from distractions and that has the necessary atmosphere of quiet and solitude, then you need look no further. The important thing is to find a space, any space, that is a refuge for you to enter fully into prayer free of distractions. After a while in the same place, entering your prayer space will be a signal to your mind and your heart that it is time for prayer, and you will begin the process of distancing yourself from the world and entering your holy space with God.

- Identify a place that you can use for daily prayer. You may choose to create a prayer space at home or in your office that includes resources for prayer and images that call you to a more prayerful attitude.

Time

With hectic schedules filled to the brim and overflowing with retreats, Masses, prayer services, and meetings, one of the first things you may be tempted to forgo is prayer. Lack of time is perhaps the most common obstacle to sustaining a regular prayer life. Because God does not demand your immediate attention, it is easy to rationalize doing other, seemingly more urgent tasks. The truth is that prayer enables you to be more available for others, rather than less. In his book *Living a Gentle, Passionate Life,* Robert Wicks addresses this prevalent issue:

> If we merely feel that our work is our prayer, reflect only when the feeling prompts us to do so or leave quiet reflection solely for unique, designated times during the day or week (Sunday?), we will then be left with an appropriately limited legacy; namely, an artificial, narrow, undemanding relationship with our inner selves and with God. (P. 49)

The truth is, making time for prayer is hard. It requires commitment and discipline. With many needs competing for your immediate attention, it is easy to get to the end of the day having spent little or no quality time connecting with God. The programming aspects of ministry are important, and responding to the endless stream of crises and pastoral concerns is necessary, but these responses should flow naturally out of a relationship with the living God. Speaking of this relationship between ministry and prayer, Henri Nouwen writes:

> The discipline of leading all our people with their struggles into the gentle and humble heart of God is the discipline of prayer as well as the discipline of ministry. As long as ministry only means that we worry a lot

about people and their problems; as long as it means an endless number of activities we can hardly coordinate, we are still very much dependent on our own narrow and anxious heart. But when our worries are led to the heart of God and there become prayer, then ministry and prayer become two manifestations of the same all-embracing love of God. (*The Way of the Heart*, p. 70)

The lives of campus ministers can often lack routine. When the bell rings at 3:00 p.m., your day is often about to peak. For prayer, you must find the time of day that works best for you. If you prefer to pray in the evenings, that is fine, but just be sure to guard that time as you would any other appointment. Mornings work well for some, because it is one of the few times of day they can control. Whether you take time before school starts or at the beginning of your school day before everything gets rolling, mornings may be the only time you can consistently take time for being with God. You may wish to look at the week ahead and schedule your prayer time for the week, including weekends. This enables you to block out time with God. By treating your prayer time as you would any other important appointment, you make spending time with God a priority in your ministry.

- Over the next few weeks, experiment with different times for your daily prayer. After trying a few different times, commit yourself to one time every day that will be your prayer time—and stick to it. In a month, evaluate how that time is working for you. Whatever time you choose, try to spend at least thirty minutes in prayer.

Prayer Ways

Endless methods and techniques for prayer from our Catholic Tradition are at your disposal. Over time, you may wish to experiment with several of these methods and find which ones work best for you. For example, a form of prayer that may have worked well for you when you were a teenager may no longer serve you as an adult. This does not mean God has abandoned you; instead, it might signal that the time for a change of format or method has arrived. Many resources about prayer are available, but perhaps the best would be to talk it over with a trusted spiritual guide or mentor. Finding the best form and expression of prayer for your personality type is necessary in developing a lifelong relationship of prayer.

- There are countless resources for your personal prayer life. You may choose to begin your prayer time with the Liturgy of the Hours or by praying the rosary. What is important is to develop a routine. Do not be afraid to evaluate how well your prayer is nourishing your personal faith life. Experiment with different prayer styles until you find one that works for you.

Spiritual Direction

There is seldom a successful athlete who has not had, or at one time did not have, a coach of some kind. As human beings, we sometimes have a difficult time looking at our lives objectively. We need a coach, someone who can look from the outside into our spiritual life. If you have never had a spiritual coach, or spiritual director, before, you may be thinking: What is a spiritual director? What would we talk about? These are normal questions.

A spiritual director is someone you choose to accompany you along your spiritual journey. Although you may have other companions, the function of your director is to watch for the movements of God in your life and prayer and to offer guidance, encouragement, and clarity. A good spiritual director has walked the road ahead of you and, although not having had your exact experiences, is trained to notice the characteristic movements of God's Spirit in the soul. Do not worry about what to talk about. Your spiritual director should provide you with plenty of questions and topics for discussion. Your director will usually require you to commit yourself to having some element of a regular prayer life and will want to discuss the dynamics of your prayer relationship with God.

There are as many different types of spiritual directors as there are people seeking direction. Finding one who meshes with your personality and spirituality may take some time, but success and longevity in ministry depend on how seriously you take the commitment to spiritual growth.

- If you do not currently have a spiritual director or a person with whom you regularly discuss your faith life, begin the process of finding such a person. Many retreat centers provide spiritual direction. In addition, your diocesan office might have a list of available spiritual directors.

Diverse Support Network

A healthy, diverse support network is a group or association of friends, colleagues, and mentors who affirm your heart's passions, challenge you when you seem to be off course, and encourage you when you lose hope. It is your responsibility to create this support team. It is not complicated, with only a few simple components. Understand that these will come together gradually. Although having this support network in place is important, remember that building a support group takes time and will develop over the years. The key is to be constantly on the lookout for individuals who may serve as valuable resources and help you along your journey with Christ.

In addition to spiritual direction, an essential element of the campus minister's support network is to maintain or create healthy, life-giving friendships that nurture your heart and soul away from school. The journey of life is not meant to be lived in isolation. We were created to exist in relationships, with God and with others. In the face of the many pressing needs of ministry is a temptation to sacrifice these supportive relationships. This may happen for a couple of reasons. First is that friendships, like any relationships, take energy, something that exists in short supply as the school year moves on. Second, we fail to give our personal relationships the priority they deserve. We may be afraid that others will consider us lazy or uncommitted if we take our personal lives, outside of ministry, seriously.

In a culture of burgeoning workaholism, setting firm boundaries helps keep you balanced and your ministries healthy. Achieving that balance takes time and involves a bit of trial and error. That balance is, however, necessary for your happiness and wholeness in ministry. Without having a safe place to let your guard down and take off your minister hat among close friends, you will slowly lose the excitement, creativity, and joy you once had.

For ministers who are married and have families, those with whom you live and whom you love are the bedrock of your support system. Often they know you better than you know yourself and can see when you need an encouraging word. They are often the first with whom you want to share your successes and the first you trust to accept you when you fail. Because ministry has a way of creeping in on every available moment you have, it is important, early on, to decide how much undistracted time you and your family need. Communicating this to the proper members of your ministry team and school community will enable those to whom you minister help you honor your commitments at school and at home. As you protect this sacred time at home with your family, you and those to whom you minister will observe your greater capacity to be fully present when you are with them. Rather than being selfish, this manner of establishing healthy boundaries honors your family and your school community.

Know Yourself

In 1 Corinthians 12:12–26, Saint Paul tells us that the Body of Christ is one, though made up of many parts. Ministers are complex wholes composed of both good and bad past experiences, gifts and shortcomings, wheat and weeds. What you bring to your ministry is all of who you are—the good, the bad, and the ugly. Identifying your gifts is important: In which areas of your life has God blessed you? Which parts of the ministry program most excite you? Which parts are your least favorite? The answers to these questions can provide you with information about your natural gifts. You may consider using a personality inventory or similar assessment tool that can provide you with valuable feedback regarding your strengths and weaknesses, likes and dislikes.

Often ministers spend much of their time working outside their gift areas because of perceived obligations. Examining the origins of such expectations is important. Are the expectations self-imposed, or are they authentic expectations that your administrators have? You may want to discuss your job description formally with clearly identified expectations. This will enable you to go home at the end of the day, breathing easy, knowing whether you have done what is required of you.

- Take some time in a prayerful atmosphere to make a gift inventory. Write down all your gifts, talents, and strengths in one column. Then, in another column next to each gift or strength, write the area or areas of your ministry in which you can use those gifts. You may wish to discuss this inventory with your spiritual director. Other members of your support network can help shed light on ways you use more of your gifts in your ministry without necessarily having to add or subtract any programs or ministries.

Time Away

One of the hazards of ministry is that ministers are always on call. Especially in an era of cell phones, e-mail, and pagers, being accessible has never been easier. In the same manner, being distracted has never been easier. Making, and taking, time away from ministry is essential. Through retreats, ministers can recharge their spiritual batteries and return to ministry with a renewed sense of faith. Vacation time spent traveling, visiting friends, working around the house, or simply resting in a hammock and reading a good book can refresh and help make you more complete.

To have a meaningful retreat or a refreshing vacation, you need to establish the boundaries of your time away. These boundaries at first will be hard to enforce. Perhaps you will feel guilty or selfish because you need to be assertive about your personal space and boundaries. Reflecting on the ministry of Jesus may be helpful in this regard. Jesus frequently took time away from his Apostles and the crowds and went off to lonely places to have time for personal reflection, prayer, and solitude. Even Jesus was not free of the divine guilt trip from those close to him: "Lord, where have you been? The crowds are hungry!" "Jesus, the people need you." Inspired and confirmed in his mission and purpose, Jesus simply responded by getting back to doing his Father's work.

Retreats

Taking time away from your ministry for deep reflection and prayer renews your passion and refreshes your vision. Just as bringing the students away for times of rest and recreation is necessary, so too must you take extended time to be in God's presence. During those times, you can more clearly and easily hear the voice of God.

Those times of extended silence and solitude are necessary to revitalize your spirit, refocus your vision, and rest your mind and body. Often, not until you enter into those times of retreat do you fully realize how tired and spent you are. In times like those, it is perfectly natural to spend a significant amount of time early in your retreat catching up on some much-needed sleep and rest. Only when your body is rested do you have the energy needed to actively listen for God's voice in your heart.

This time for retreat is essential to your effectiveness as a campus minister. Just as your house needs a deep spring cleaning once a year, so too is it necessary, in addition to the normal disciplines of your prayer life, to include a yearly personal retreat.

- If a personal retreat is not already on your calendar and in your budget for the coming year, make a point to talk with your administrators about adding it.

Vacation

For ministers, it is crucial to be able to be away from ministry for time with family, friends, or self for the enjoyment of a vacation. It is important to rest and mentally and emotionally disconnect from life at school. Plenty of other people are available to handle ministry emergencies or crises. It would be wise to notify your administrators and faculty members (and possibly your ministry team) of who the emergency contacts are when you are on vacation or retreat. Protecting your time away is essential, and only you can protect your healthy boundaries—you cannot count on anyone else to create and protect them for you.

- Schedule your vacation time at the beginning of the year and stick to that schedule. Be flexible in case of a major emergency.

Servant Ministry

Campus ministers are servants. They serve the student body as part of the mission of Christ and the Church. It is essential for ministers, sharing in Jesus's ministry, to possess the same attitude of Christ, which was that of a servant (Phil. 2:7).

A temptation exists to see our ministries as merely jobs. Although this is partially true, a more fitting perspective views campus ministry as a service to the Church, as a calling rather than a career. As we perform our various tasks and projects with greater ease and confidence, we are tempted to overly credit ourselves with the effectiveness of the ministry, when in reality it is always God's grace working through us.

Viewing ministry as a calling, rather than as a job or career, allows us to see the work of our hands as a response to God's invitation. Even in the midst of our most creative ideas, we must remember that Christian ministry is always God's initiative. In the end, our effectiveness will be measured not by the number and novelty of the programs offered but by our willingness to answer God's call to service each day.

In his seminal work on Christian ministry in the modern era, *In the Name of Jesus*, Henri Nouwen states that ministers are faced with the temptation to be spectacular. He suggests that ministers, faced with the pressing and urgent needs of God's people, end up desiring popularity and status as one who can get things done—be successful. The solution, Nouwen says, is collegiality, confession, and forgiveness.

Our daily listening to God's soft voice sustains in us the attitude of service. God reminds us why we first chose to accept his invitation to a life of ministry. Our commitment to the spiritual disciplines of self-examination, prayer, and experiencing God's mercy through reconciliation will keep us from becoming jaded and will enable us and our ministries to remain joyful, creative, and compassionate.

Conclusion

Your spirituality as a campus minister encompasses the whole person. Attending to your body, soul, heart, and mind enables you to serve God's people wholeheartedly rather than merely serving out of a sense of obligation or in a chronic state of fatigue. Remember that you are not less important than those you serve. Confident that you are made in the image and likeness of God, you can begin organizing your life around your priorities and maintaining a healthy balance among prayer, rest, relationships, and ministry. This balanced and spiritual approach to structuring your life and ministry gives you ready access to the various sources of energy and renewal in your life. As the issues in the lives of today's teens grow more complex, it has never been more important for campus ministers to have a spirituality with the depth and breadth to meet today's pastoral demands adequately.

Eight-Day Prayer Experience for Campus Ministers

Below you will find an eight-day prayer journey for your personal life. Each prayer begins with the Scriptures, followed by reflection and prayer. We encourage you to set aside a regular time—preferably thirty minutes—for eight days to enter into this prayer. Find someplace quiet in which you can be alone and away from distractions. Take time to reflect on the Scriptures as you pray. You might also wish to consider keeping a journal of your prayer experiences. This resource is intended to start your prayer process; our hope is that you will continue to nourish your spiritual life with regular prayer past those eight days.

Day One: Be Still
Scripture Passage: Psalm 46

Take time to prayerfully sit with this Scripture passage. After reading it silently and slowly, read it again out loud, listening to the words as you speak them. After a moment of silence, read it again out loud, paying special attention to any words or phrases that stand out.

Questions for Journaling and Reflection

- As you enter into this time of prayerful solitude, what part of you resists slowing down enough to be present?
- What part of your heart yearns for silence and renewal?
- As you pray today, what area or areas of your life are the least still?
- What issues or things in your life do you need to invite God into?
- What grace do you need from God today?

Prayer

Loving God, so often I am tempted to believe I am in control, forgetting that you are my God. Thank you for being patient, for loving me at times like those, and for gently calling me back to the peace that comes with complete surrender. Amen.

Day Two: What Do You Want Me to Do for You?
Scripture Passage: Mark 10:46–52

Take time to prayerfully sit with this Scripture passage. After reading it silently and slowly, read it again out loud, listening to the words as you speak them. After a moment of silence, read it again out loud, paying special attention to any words or phrases that stand out.

Questions for Journaling and Reflection

- When have I felt unworthy of God's attention or love?
- How has that affected my relationship with God?
- What do I want God to do for me now?
- What prayers has God answered? What graces has he given me?
- In what areas of my life and ministry could I benefit from clearer vision?

Prayer

Creator God, at times my vision is blurred, and seeing you at work in my life and in the lives of those I serve is difficult. Give me new eyes to see your often gentle movements in my heart and among those to whom I minister. Amen.

Day Three: You Are My Beloved
Scripture Passage: Mark 1:9–11

Take time to prayerfully sit with this Scripture passage. After reading it silently and slowly, read it again out loud, listening to the words as you speak them. After a moment of silence, read it again out loud, paying special attention to any words or phrases that stand out.

Questions for Journaling and Reflection

- When I think about how much God loves me, what comes to mind that makes me want to disprove that? What part of me resists God's love? Why?
- Who in my life most reflects God's unconditional love for me?
- For whom have I been a presence of God's unconditional love?
- If I really ministered from and lived in the place of knowing that God loved me no matter what, how would my ministry look? How would my life look?
- Whom specifically do I need to share God's love with at school or at home?

Prayer

Father, at Jesus's baptism, you affirmed his identity and empowered him for his mission. When I forget who I am, and whose I am, allow me to experience the affirmation and encouragement I need to continue to serve in your name. Amen.

Day Four: Today I Must Stay at Your House
Scripture Passage: Luke 19:1–10

Take time to prayerfully sit with this Scripture passage. After reading it silently and slowly, read it again out loud, listening to the words as you speak them. After a moment of silence, read it again out loud, paying special attention to any words or phrases that stand out.

Questions for Journaling and Reflection

- What things in my life prevent me from "tree climbing" to see the Lord?
- In what ways can I be more like Zacchaeus, who went out of his way to see Jesus?
- What parts of my life am I ashamed for Jesus to see?
- What "possessions" can I part with to make more room for Jesus in my "house"?

Prayer

Jesus, my teacher and savior, help me be more like Zacchaeus, who troubled himself to see you. Help me to make more room in my life for you by letting go of the things that stand between us. May this draw me closer to you and the students I serve. Amen.

Day Five: The Better Part
Scripture Passage: Luke 10:38–42

Take time to prayerfully sit with this Scripture passage. After reading it silently and slowly, read it again out loud, listening to the words as you speak them. After a moment of silence, read it again out loud, paying special attention to any words or phrases that stand out.

Questions for Journaling and Reflection

- At this time in my ministry, whom do I resonate with the most: Martha or Mary?
- What does choosing the "better part" mean for my personal life?
- How might I choose the better part in my ministry?
- In what ways is God calling me to a greater balance between active ministry and contemplative prayer?
- How can I more fully integrate my prayer life with active ministry? How can I help my fellow teachers and the students do the same?

Prayer

God of justice, you call me to a life of prayer and service. Give me the grace to know when I need to seek you more deeply in contemplation and when I need to seek you more actively through service to my brothers and sisters. Amen.

Day Six: A Tiny, Whispering Sound
Scripture Passage: 1 Kings 19:1–18

Take time to prayerfully sit with this Scripture passage. After reading it silently and slowly, read it again out loud, listening to the words as you speak them. After a moment of silence, read it again out loud, paying special attention to any words or phrases that stand out.

Questions for Journaling and Reflection

- In what ways have I, like Elijah, been most zealous for the Lord?
- In which areas of my life do I most need renewal spiritually? emotionally? physically?
- How have I heard God's voice before in my life?
- What temptations do I face to resist waiting in prayer for God's voice?
- When have I mistaken the sound of "thunder" for the voice of the Lord?
- What actions could I begin taking to seek renewal in the areas of my life that are tired and in need of healing rest?

Prayer

My God and strength, in the midst of serving you, I become tired and weary at times. When the journey to you seems long and impossible, remind me to be gentle with myself, showing me how to care for my body, mind, and spirit. May my efforts at ministry always be a response to your voice of love spoken to me in prayer. Amen.

Day Seven: Plans for Your Well-Being
Scripture Passage: Jer. 29:11–14

Take time to prayerfully sit with this Scripture passage. After reading it silently and slowly, read it again out loud, listening to the words as you speak them. After a moment of silence, read it again out loud, paying special attention to any words or phrases that stand out.

Questions for Journaling and Reflection

- In what areas of my life am I most hopeful? least hopeful?
- How much time do I spend worrying about the future?
- Do I really believe God has a hopeful future for me? If not, what keeps me from trusting God?
- Do I really feel that God is listening to me when I pray to him? How can I be a better listener when I am praying?
- What aspects of my ministry offer my students a compelling future full of hope?

Prayer

Lord, allow me to let go of all useless fear and anxiety, all worry and preoccupation with things I have little or no control over. Keep me rooted in the present moment, hopeful and trusting that your providence extends over my past and present and into my future. Amen.

Day Eight: Leave Your Nets
Scripture Passage: Matthew 4:18–22

Take time to prayerfully sit with this Scripture passage. After reading it silently and slowly, read it again out loud, listening to the words as you speak them. After a moment of silence, read it again out loud, paying special attention to any words or phrases that stand out.

Questions for Journaling and Reflection

- When did I first feel called, or drawn, to follow Christ?
- Who was the fisher who reeled me in? How did he or she do it?
- What were the "nets" I was told to leave behind?
- Have I ever regretted leaving my nets behind to follow Christ? Why?
- Whom has Christ called to join me in ministry?
- In what ways can I become a better fisher on campus?

Prayer

Christ Jesus, thank you for the privilege of sharing in your ministry to young people. When times get hard and I am tempted to return to my old nets, show me the adventure that is still ahead of me and allow me to feel that I am never in this boat alone, that you are with me at all times. Amen.

Appendix

Resources

Print Resources

Liturgy and Prayer

Alonso, Tony, Laurie Delgatto, and Robert Feduccia. *As Morning Breaks and Evening Sets*. Winona, MN: Saint Mary's Press, 2005.

Arsenault, Jane E., and Jean R. Cedor. *Guided Meditations for Youth on Sacramental Life*. Winona, MN: Saint Mary's Press, 1993.

Ballenger, Barbara, ed. *Prayer Without Borders: Celebrating Global Wisdom*. Baltimore: Catholic Relief Services, 2004.

Bishops' Committee on the Liturgy. *Catholic Household Blessings and Prayers*. Washington, DC: United States Conference of Catholic Bishops, 1989.

Brown, Therese, Laurie Delgatto, Christine Schmertz Navarro, and Mary Shrader. *Total Catechesis: Catechetical Sessions on Liturgy and the Sacraments*. Winona, MN: Saint Mary's Press, 2004.

Calderone-Stewart, Lisa-Marie. In Touch with the Word series. Winona, MN: Saint Mary's Press, 1996–1999.

Christian Prayer: The Liturgy of the Hours. New York: Catholic Book Publishing Company, 1976.

Days of the Lord: The Liturgical Year series. Collegeville, MN: Liturgical Press, 1993.

Delgatto, Laurie, and Mary Shrader. *Total Catechesis: Catechetical Sessions on Christian Prayer*. Winona, MN: Saint Mary's Press, 2004.

East, Tom. *Total Youth Ministry: Ministry Resources for Prayer and Worship*. Winona, MN: Saint Mary's Press, 2004.

Egeberg, Gary. *Stations for Teens: Meditations on the Death and Resurrection of Jesus*. Winona, MN: Saint Mary's Press, 1999.

Enzler, Clarence. *Everyone's Way of the Cross*. Notre Dame, IN: Ave Maria Press, 1996.

Foley, Kathleen, and Peggy O'Leary. *Daily Prayer in the Classroom: Interactive Daily Prayer*. Collegeville, MN: Liturgical Press, 2002.

Gaeta, Francis X. *With You Always: Daily Meditations on the Gospels*. Notre Dame, IN: Ave Maria Press, 2000.

Green, Thomas H. *Opening to God: A Guide to Prayer*. Notre Dame, IN: Ave Maria Press, 1977.

Hoffman, Elizabeth, ed. *The Liturgy Documents: A Parish Resource.* Chicago: Liturgy Training Publications, 1991.

International Commission on English in the Liturgy. *The Rites of the Catholic Church.* Collegeville, MN: Liturgical Press, 1991.

———. *Sacramentary.* New York: Catholic Book Publishing Company, 1985.

Iwanski, Sandra. *Keeping Time: Praying Advent Throughout the School Day.* Winona, MN: Saint Mary's Press, 2006.

Keating, Thomas. *Intimacy with God.* New York: Crossroad, 1994.

Klein, Patricia. *Worship Without Words: The Signs and Symbols of Our Faith.* Brewster, MA: Paraclete Press, 2000.

Koch, Carl. *Garden of a Thousand Gates: Pathways to Prayer.* Winona, MN: Saint Mary's Press, 1998.

Kreeft, Peter. *Prayer for Beginners.* San Francisco: Ignatius Press, 2000.

Krupp, Laure L. *Gather Faithfully: Inviting Teens into Liturgical Ministries Participant's Booklet* and *Leader's Guide.* Winona, MN: Saint Mary's Press, 2006.

Leinin, Ronald. *Encountering Jesus in the Gospels and Daily Life.* Carlsbad, CA: Canticle Books, 2000.

Link, Mark. *The Psalms for Today.* Allen, TX: Tabor Publishing, 1989.

Loecher, Joanne. *Faith Experiences for Teens and Parents: Taking Time Together.* Winona, MN: Saint Mary's Press, 1996.

Lysik, David, ed. *The Liturgy Documents: A Parish Resource.* Chicago: Liturgy Training Publications, 1991.

National Federation for Catholic Youth Ministry (NFCYM). *From Age to Age: The Challenge of Worship with Adolescents.* Washington, DC: NFCYM, 1997.

Regan, S. Kevin. *20 More Teen Prayer Services.* Mystic, CT: Twenty-Third Publications, 1994.

Rushing, Rebecca. *Teaching Activities Manual for The Catholic Youth Prayer Book.* Winona, MN: Saint Mary's Press, 2006.

Searle, Mark. *Liturgy Made Simple.* Collegeville, MN: Liturgical Press, 1981.

Shrader, Mary, Laure L. Krupp, Robert Feduccia Jr., and Matthew J. Miller. *The Catholic Youth Prayer Book.* Winona, MN: Saint Mary's Press, 2006.

Singer-Towns, Brian, et al. *The Catholic Faith Handbook for Youth.* Winona, MN: Saint Mary's Press, 2004.

———. *Vibrant Worship with Youth: Keys for Implementing "From Age to Age: The Challenge of Worship with Adolescents."* Winona, MN: Saint Mary's Press, 2000.

Spirit and Song: A Seeker's Guide for Liturgy and Prayer. Portland, OR: OCP Publications, 1997.

Sweet, Marilyn J. *Preparing to Celebrate with Youth.* Collegeville, MN: Liturgical Press, 1997.

Thiron, Rita. *Preparing Parish Liturgies: A Guide to Resources.* Collegeville, MN: Liturgical Press, 2004.

United States Catholic Conference (USCC). *Catechism of the Catholic Church.* Washington, DC: USCC, 1994.

———. *Renewing the Vision: A Framework for Catholic Youth Ministry.* Washington, DC: USCC, 1997.

United States Conference of Catholic Bishops (USCCB). *General Instruction of the Roman Missal.* Washington, DC: USCCB, 2003.

Retreats

Braden-Whartenby, Geri, and Joan Finn Connelly. *One-Day Retreats for Senior High Youth.* Winona, MN: Saint Mary's Press, 1997.

Christie, Les. *Unfinished Sentences.* Grand Rapids, MI: Zondervan/Youth Specialties, 2000.

———. *What If . . . ?* Grand Rapids, MI: Zondervan/Youth Specialties, 1996.

Furlan, Mark J. *Creating a Successful Youth Retreat: Eight Steps to a Well-Planned Experience.* Chicago: Thomas More Association, 2003.

Grgic, Bob. *Resources for Outdoor Retreats: Journey into Nature, Journey into the Heart.* Winona, MN: Saint Mary's Press, 1994.

Hakowski, Maryann. *Getaways with God: Youth Retreats for Any Schedule.* Winona, MN: Saint Mary's Press, 2003.

———. *Vine and Branches,* vols. 1 and 2. Winona, MN: Saint Mary's Press, 1991.

Keller, Julia Ann. *Retreats: Deepening the Spirituality of Girls.* Voices series. Winona, MN: Saint Mary's Press, 2002.

Kielbasa, Marilyn, ed. HELP series: *Retreat Ideas for Ministry with Young Teens.* Winona, MN: Saint Mary's Press, 2001.

McGlaun, Steven C., ed., et al. *The Covenant Retreat: A Discernment Experience for High School Seniors.* Winona, MN: Saint Mary's Press, 2005.

Oestreicher, Mark. *Every Picture Tells a Story: 48 Evocative Photographs for Inspiring Reaction and Reflection.* El Cajon, CA: Youth Specialties, 2002.

Polich, Laurie. *Help! I'm a Small-Group Leader: 50 Ways to Lead Teenagers into Animated and Purposeful Discussion.* Grand Rapids, MI: Zondervan/Youth Specialties, 1998.

Sawyer, Kieran. *Time Out: Resources for Teen Retreats.* Notre Dame, IN: Ave Maria Press, 1998.

Windley-Daoust, Jerry. *Answering God's Call to Covenant: Which Way to the Rest of Your Life?* Winona, MN: Saint Mary's Press, 2005.

Service Learning

Bright, Thomas J., Sean T. Lansing, Mike Poulin, and Joan Weber. *Total Youth Ministry: Ministry Resources for Justice and Service.* Winona, MN: Saint Mary's Press, 2004.

Cavanaugh, Ellen P. *Living the Works of Mercy: Daring Teens to Change the World.* Winona, MN: Saint Mary's Press, 2003.

DeBerri, Edward, et al. *Catholic Social Teaching: Our Best Kept Secret*. Maryknoll, NY: Orbis, 1988.

Dwyer, Judith, ed. *The New Dictionary of Catholic Social Thought*. Collegeville, MN: Liturgical Press, 1994.

Fourré, Constance. *Making the Hours Count Student Book* and *Leader's Guide*. Winona, MN: Saint Mary's Press, 2006.

Grant, Joseph. HELP series: *Justice and Service Ideas for Ministry with Young Teens*. Winona, MN: Saint Mary's Press, 2001.

Himes, Kenneth. *Responses to 101 Questions on Catholic Social Teaching*. New York: Paulist Press, 2001.

Lewis, Barbara A. *The Kid's Guide to Service Projects: Over 500 Service Ideas for Young People Who Want to Make a Difference*. Minneapolis: Free Spirit Publishing, 1995.

———. *The Kid's Guide to Social Action: How to Solve the Social Problems You Choose—and Turn Creative Thinking into Positive Action*. Minneapolis: Free Spirit Publishing, 1991.

Mich, Marvin Krier. *Catholic Social Teaching and Movements*. Mystic, CT: Twenty-Third Publications, 1998.

National Federation for Catholic Youth Ministry (NFCYM). *Environmental Justice Resource Manual*. Washington, DC: NFCYM, 1999.

O'Brien, David J., and Thomas Shannon, eds. *Catholic Social Thought: The Documentary Heritage*. Maryknoll, NY: Orbis, 1992.

O'Connell, Francis Hunt. *Giving and Growing: A Student's Guide for Service Projects*. Winona, MN: Saint Mary's Press, 1990.

Leadership

Eckert, Ann Marie, and Maria Sánchez-Keane. *Total Youth Ministry: Ministry Resources for Youth Leadership Development*. Winona, MN: Saint Mary's Press, 2004.

Kielbasa, Marilyn. *Total Youth Ministry: Ministry Resources for Pastoral Care*. Winona, MN: Saint Mary's Press, 2004.

McCarty, Robert J. *Teen to Teen: Responding to Peers in Crisis*. Winona, MN: Saint Mary's Press, 1996.

Mercadante, Frank. *Growing Teen Disciples: Strategies for Really Effective Youth Ministry*. Winona, MN: Saint Mary's Press, 1998.

Provencher, Maureen. *Never Too Young to Lead: Developing Leadership in Young Adolescents*. Winona, MN: Saint Mary's Press, 2006.

Reynolds, Brian. *A Chance to Serve: A Leader's Manual for Peer Ministry*. Winona, MN: Saint Mary's Press, 1983.

Reynolds, Sean P. *Multiply the Ministry: A Practical Guide for Grassroots Ministry Empowerment*. Winona, MN: Saint Mary's Press, 2006.

United States Conference of Catholic Bishops (USCCB). *Co-Workers in the Vineyard of the Lord*. Washington, DC: USCCB, 2005.

Spirituality of the Minister

Brother Lawrence. *The Practice of the Presence of God*. New Kensington, PA: Whitaker House, 1982.

Clark, Chap. *Hurt: Inside the World of Today's Teenagers*. Grand Rapids, MI: Baker Academic, 2004.

González-Balado, José Luis. *Mother Teresa: In My Own Words*. New York: Gramercy Books, 1996.

Nouwen, Henri J. M. *In the Name of Jesus: Reflections on Christian Leadership*. New York: Crossroad, 1996.

————. *The Way of the Heart: Desert Spirituality and Contemporary Ministry*. San Francisco: HarperSanFrancisco, 1991.

Palmer, Parker. *The Courage to Teach: Exploring the Inner Landscape of a Teacher's Life*. San Francisco: Jossey-Bass, 1997.

Wicks, Robert J., ed. *Handbook of Spirituality for Ministers*. Mahwah, NJ: Paulist Press, 1995.

Yaconelli, Michael. *Messy Dangerous Wonder*. Colorado Springs, CO: Navpress, 1998.

————. *Spirituality*. Grand Rapids, MI: Zondervan, 2002.

General Campus Ministry

Hallahan, Angela, ed. *Doing Great Campus Ministry*. Notre Dame, IN: Ave Maria Press, 2003.

Nanko, Carmen. *Campus Ministry: Identity, Mission and Praxis*. Washington, DC: National Catholic Education Association, 2001.

Shaughnessy, Mary Angela. *Campus Ministry and the Law: A Guide for the Minister*. Washington, DC: National Catholic Education Association, 2003.

Smith, Christian, and Melinda Lundquist Denton. *Soul Searching: The Religious and Spiritual Lives of American Teenagers*. New York: Oxford University Press, 2005.

Wermert, Dennis. *Connecting on Campus: Designing and Sustaining Effective High School Campus Ministry*. Washington, DC: National Catholic Education Association, 2004.

Acknowledgments

at *www.vatican.va/archive/hist_councils/ii_vatican_council/documents/vat-ii_const_
19641121_lumen-gentium_en.html,* accessed August 20, 2006.

The quotation under "Theology" on page 68 is from "A Vision of Faith for Young Adults," at the Secretariat for Family, Laity, Women, and Youth Web site, *www.usccb.org/laity/ygadult/sdengpart2.shtml,* accessed August 20, 2006.

The excerpts on pages 82, 82, and 83–84 are from *The Way of the Heart,* by Henri J.M. Nouwen (New York: Ballantine Books, 1983), pages 20, 72–73, and 70, respectively. Copyright © 1981 by Henri J.M. Nouwen.

The quotation on page 83 is from *Living a Gentle, Passionate Life,* by Robert Wicks (Mahwah, NJ: Paulist Press, 1998), page 49. Copyright © 1998 by Robert Wicks.

To view copyright terms and conditions for Internet materials cited here, log on to the home pages for the referenced Web sites.

During this book's preparation, all citations, facts, figures, names, addresses, telephone numbers, Internet URLs, and other pieces of information cited within were verified for accuracy. The authors and Saint Mary's Press staff have made every attempt to reference current and valid sources, but we cannot guarantee the content of any source, and we are not responsible for any changes that may have occurred since our verification. If you find an error in, or have a question or concern about, any of the information or sources listed within, please contact Saint Mary's Press.

Photo Credits